RHYTHMS OF GRACE

Harrison House

Shippensburg, PA

HARRISON HOUSE BOOKS BY DUANE SHERIFF

Our Union with Christ

Better Together

Counter Culture

Erasing Offense

RHYTHMS OF GRACE

EXPERIENCING FREEDOM FROM FEAR, WORRY, AND STRESS

DUANE SHERIFF

Published by Harrison House Publishers
Shippensburg, PA 17257

ISBN 13 TP: 978-1-6675-0273-1

ISBN 13 eBook: 978-1-6675-0274-8

For Worldwide Distribution, Printed in the U.S.A.

1 2 3 4 5 6 7 8 / 27 26 25 24 23

CONTENTS

INTRODUCTION

God doesn't want us walking through life overloaded. His Word makes it clear that we are too blessed to be stressed. And while there is a certain amount of hardship that comes to everyone in this life, God has not asked any of us to shoulder the burden of anxiety, worry, or fear.

Too often, believers become overwhelmed by life because they have picked up something God never intended for them to carry. I get it. Living in our loud, busy world is challenging. Sometimes, even making a living and putting food on the table can be burdensome—not to mention the stress of making marriage work or raising children (or in some cases a spouse—I know Sue had to raise me for a season, I'm doing much better today); dealing with the backlash of government injunctions and mandates; and processing the words of corrupt officials and agenda-pushing news anchors. Add to that people intent on getting offended, workplace shutdowns and job losses, escalating tensions over the economy, and all the other things that shout for our attention, and it can feel overwhelming to be light in a culture of death and darkness. Even learning to turn off all the noise and listen to the still, small voice of the Lord can be difficult.

Yet God has commanded us to rest. He has called each of His children to a life of faith, not fear. To a life of peace, not stress. In Matthew chapter eleven, Jesus invites all who are heavy laden, overloaded, and overwhelmed by life to come to Him. He reveals the unforced rhythms of God's grace that deliver us from fear and give us the tools we need to overcome the challenges of this life.

> *Are you tired? Worn out? Burned out on religion? Come to me. Get away with me and you'll recover your life. I'll show you how to take a real rest. Walk with me and you'll recover your life. I'll show you how to take a real rest. Walk with me and work with me—watch how I do it. Learn the unforced rhythms of grace. I won't lay anything heavy or ill-fitting on you. Keep company with me and you'll learn to live freely and lightly.*
>
> Matthew 11:28-30 (MSG)

I hear you saying, "That's a beautiful sentiment, but how do we do that?" Well, this book exists to answer that very question. Join me as we dive deep into these Scriptures and learn to cast our anxiety on the Lord—to let go of the cares of this life that produce burden and stress, and rest in the knowledge of His love and care for us (see 1 Pet. 5:7).

Chapter One

DESIGNED FOR REST

The whole earth is at rest and is quiet;
they break forth into singing.

Isaiah 14:7

Like all of creation, we need to learn to rest. When God created the world, the Bible tells us He worked six days and rested on the seventh (see Gen. 2:2). It's not that God was tired after fashioning the universe and in need of physical rest or a well-deserved vacation. He rested because His work was complete; it was perfect. Nothing else needed to be added to or taken from it. Like a painter adding the final stroke to his newest masterpiece, when God created man, He saw that everything He made was very good (see Gen. 1:31). And everything He had imagined was complete. All that remained was to enjoy the work of His hands. So, God rested.

Man was to follow that example and work six days, then rest on the seventh. Rest was a sustaining practice. It was a call to spend time with God, to enjoy the work of God's hands, and to be rejuvenated in both body and mind. Later, when God gave the law in Exodus 20, He told Israel to *"remember the Sabbath day, to keep it holy"* (Exod. 20:8). Israel was to look back and remember that, in original creation, God had ceased from His labor and called us into rest—into relationship—with Him. And in that remembering, they were to recognize that while something in God's original design was lost in Adam's sin, God would one day restore all things and return mankind to His Sabbath rest.

When Jesus invited the overwhelmed and heavy-laden to find rest in Him in Matthew 11, He was calling His hearers to return to God's original design. God wants each and every one of us—regardless of the stage of life we're in or where we are in relationship with Him—to be at rest. But too often, we exist far below God's design. We allow worldly pressure and the cares of this life to produce anxiety, worry, and fear in our hearts. Are you stressed? Are you afraid of the future or worried about tomorrow? Jesus has invited you to join Him in these rhythms of grace and discover what makes a life of rest possible.

Jesus' invitation to come to Him and find rest is often used in conjunction with salvation in which Jesus removes the burden of our sin and extends complete forgiveness. While that certainly applies and is our first step in a life of rest, this invitation is a profound promise that God, in Christ, is bringing us back to His original plan for humanity. It is a call to cease from our own self-righteousness and personal holiness to have relationship with God and now receive of His grace found in Jesus. Rest in the finished work of the cross. When you are not at rest with God, finding rest from the challenges of life are impossible. Only in rest and peace with God can we now find rest and peace in a world of chaos.

But what exactly did Jesus mean when He invited those who were *"heavy laden"*? Have you ever seen a book or

This invitation is a profound promise that God, in Christ, is bringing us back to His original plan for humanity.

storage shelf so overloaded that it has begun to sag? What happens if that weight isn't redistributed? Eventually, the weight of the books either warps the shelves or breaks them. That's what it means to be heavy laden. The heavy-laden heart is overloaded. It is burdened and weighed down to the point that one more thing could overwhelm it or break it. And many good, Spirit-filled believers feel this way. They are overwhelmed by life's challenges, stressed by circumstances that seem to be warring against them, and so overcharged that they react to every little thing that comes along as if their life hung in the balance. They've ceased to relate properly to their problems and have allowed that stress to overflow in the way they treat others and even respond to God.

God does not want us living a life of stress. He never intended for us to carry the weight of anxiety, worry, or fear. Our bodies and minds weren't created for it. We have to learn to let those things go. To avoid being overloaded. And when we discover that we are feeling overwhelmed, we must learn to unload the things from our lives that cause stress, worry, and anxiety.

FIRST RHYTHM OF GRACE

Jesus said, ***"Come to Me****, all you who labor and are heavy laden, and I will give you rest"* (Matt. 11:28). Notice that Jesus' invitation is to a Person. Not a doctrine or teaching. Not a philosophy. A Person. God made flesh. No one in history has (or could) make such a profound claim. Though false messiahs and religious leaders all over the world offer new doctrines, weird teachings, and strange philosophies to help you find rest, each one relies on your work and performance. Jesus didn't offer a new philosophy. He offered Himself.

Jesus offers rest to all who come to Him in faith. If you have come to Jesus and been born again, that rest resides in your spirit. Your spirit is at peace. It is righteous and truly holy (see Eph. 4:24). And while the other parts of you—your soul and body—may not always feel restful, your spirit is *"sealed with the Holy Spirit of promise"* (Eph. 1:13). It is complete and at rest in Christ (see Col. 2:10). But to experience that peace in your daily life, you have to learn to let the best of you rule the rest of you. You have to allow your spirit to dominate, and you must let the Holy Spirit in you teach your soul and body to rest.

If you are stressed, even in the name of the Lord and your service to Him, you have picked up something God did not ask you to carry. Instead of laboring out of relationship with God, you have given yourself a spiritual hernia. The only way to overcome worry, anxiety, and fear is to embrace the unforced rhythms of God's grace that Jesus described in these verses. That's how we successfully navigate the challenges of life and learn to draw on the Holy Spirit in us.

The first rhythm of grace Jesus described in this passage is to come to Him. To experience peace, we have to come to Jesus—both in our initial salvation experience and in our everyday relationship with Him. Relationship is not a one-time experience. Unfortunately, when faced with problems, many of us forget to come to Jesus. Our senses take over, and that shifting of focus sparks anxiety. It creates fear and causes unnecessary stress in our lives. But when we develop the discipline of coming to Jesus no matter the circumstance, our lives become easier. This rhythm of grace rescues us from disaster. It protects us in trials and afflictions so that we experience God's peace and power in everything we face (see Phil. 4:7).

In 2018, Sue and I received a call that our grandson had been born dead and our daughter-in-law's life was in danger. Like any of you in a moment of crisis, we were tempted to panic. Though doctors and nurses worked feverishly to save our daughter-in-law and revive our grandson, fear tried to creep in. So, we "came unto Jesus." We turned to Him with prayers and supplications for our family's lives. We looked to Him and held tight to His Word, reminding ourselves to stay focused on His goodness so that our minds wouldn't run wild or our hearts become overwhelmed.

But when we develop the discipline of coming to Jesus no matter the circumstance, our lives become easier. This rhythm of grace rescues us from disaster.

The doctors were able to stabilize our daughter-in-law rather quickly, but it took twenty minutes to revive our grandson. Since his little brain had been without oxygen at least that long (we're not sure how long he'd been without oxygen in the uterus and birth canal), the prognosis was not good. They airlifted Baby

Urias to the nearest Neonatal Intensive Care unit, and for 21 days, our entire family and church prayed. Throughout that three weeks of bad news, small victories, setbacks, and tiny steps forward, God was faithful. We were told Urias would never walk or talk—that he wouldn't be able to feed himself and would basically spend the whole of his life as a vegetable. It was difficult to hear that report spoken over him, but we chose to believe God. God's report was greater than any doctor's report. And 21 days later, we walked out of that hospital with a healed baby boy!

Today, Urias is a happy, healthy, functioning little boy, attending school and loving life. Hallelujah! We are so thankful for God's grace and the years of disciplining ourselves to come unto Jesus and keep coming no matter what report we receive.

Hebrews 12:1-3 admonishes us to come to Jesus and stay focused on Him by *"lay*[ing] *aside every weight, and the sin which so easily ensnares us."* It tells us to *"run with endurance the race set before us, looking unto Jesus, the author and finisher of our faith... lest* [we] *become weary and discouraged in* [our] *souls."* When we're not looking unto Jesus, it's easy to become weary. Sensory input overloads our souls, and we faint in our minds. Yet how many people consider everything but the Lord when facing difficulty? How many look to Moses and the law saying, "If I just do this thing right or stop doing that, God will come through"? How many look to worldly philosophies to solve their problems? Or rely on themselves and their own strength and wisdom, instead of looking unto Jesus and applying His Word?

Let me give you an example of what I mean. My Uncle Joe was an alcoholic. Watching the enemy use alcohol to destroy Uncle Joe's life was sad. He dealt with so much pain, all because he didn't know how to come to Jesus. Uncle Joe only knew how to go to Jack Daniels. The bottle became his place of solace and refuge. He tried to drown the memories of his broken heart and deaden the pain of a life without God, but his attempts only led to more pain and loneliness. They led to unfruitfulness and, ultimately, a tragic death. Many of us have similar dependencies. Maybe not with alcohol, but in our burdens and afflictions, we've made a habit of looking to something besides Jesus for wisdom and comfort. We seek peace in movies or television. We look for rest in expensive vacations. We attempt to drown sorrow in money, food, and friends. But all we find is more stress, more pain, more fear.

We must all learn to develop the rhythm of coming to Jesus. Not only once in our initial salvation experience but daily in both the good and bad of our lives. And while the practical application of this rhythm will be different for each of us, the principle remains the same. The apostle Peter said, *"If indeed you have tasted that the Lord is gracious.* ***Coming to Him*** *as to a living stone, rejected indeed by men, but chosen by God and precious"* (1 Pet. 2:3-4).

Notice to whom Peter is talking in this verse—those who have *"tasted that the Lord is gracious."* He is talking to Christians. To those believers, he says, "Keep coming to Jesus, the living stone." Many neglect coming to Jesus in all things, and their hearts become overwhelmed. But those who choose to keep coming to Jesus find that He is indeed precious. His grace delivers them from worry, trouble, and fear.

Many are the afflictions of the righteous, but the Lord delivers him out of them all.

Psalm 34:19

Those who choose to keep coming to Jesus find that He is indeed precious.

Jesus' redemptive work should remove all tormenting fear from your life. We are at peace with God, and we have access to a peace and rest in Christ that *"surpasses all understanding"* (Rom. 5:1; Phil. 4:7). When something bad happens in your marriage or at work, remember that the Prince of Peace reigns in your heart, and choose to be dominated by Him. Go *"boldly unto the throne of grace* [not law] *to obtain mercy* [not wrath] *and find grace to help in your time of need"* (Heb. 4:16 author's paraphrase). Jesus is seated on the throne and is there for us at any time of need. Keep coming to Him. Regardless of the need, you will be met with grace and mercy.

Jesus sums this rhythm of grace nicely in John 5:39-40, *"You search the Scriptures, for in them you think you have eternal life; and these are they which testify of Me. But you are not willing to come to Me that you may have life."* As important as the scriptures are and to a believer they are vital, they do not replace relationship with Jesus but rather take us to Jesus for relationship. We are married to a person, not a book.

Chapter Two

RELATIONSHIP OVER RELIGION

Stand fast therefore in the liberty by which Christ has made us free, and do not be entangled again with a ***yoke of bondage***.

Galatians 5:1

The next rhythm of grace Jesus gave in Matthew chapter eleven is to "*take* [His] *yoke upon you and learn of Me for I am gentle and lowly of heart and you will find rest for your souls*" (Matt. 11:29). We have to be yoked up to Jesus. Like two oxen yoked and pulling together in the same direction, Jesus wants each member of His Bride to be yoked and remain yoked to Him. He wants us to move as one, to pull together through the challenges of life as partners in grace (which is Jesus' part) and faith (which is our part).

Nothing causes worry, anxiety, and fear in a Christian's life like guilt, shame, and condemnation. And nothing breeds condemnation like religion and the law. Religion is choosing to be yoked up to something besides Jesus. In Christian circles, it's being yoked to the law of Moses and looking to that law, with all its rules and regulations, for life and relationship with God. Or looking to the law for acceptance and blessings from God. The law demands perfection. *"For whoever shall keep the whole law, and yet offend in one point, he is guilty of all"* (James 2:10 KJV). God—through the grace that is in Christ—asks for relationship, not perfection.

Under the law, to be blessed or accepted, you must keep all of it—not some of it, most of it, or more than your neighbor. To be saved or blessed by the yoke of the law one must keep all of it. If broken in one point, you become guilty of breaking all of it. Laboring under such a burden of performance-based acceptance with God becomes overwhelming. Being yoked to Jesus brings grace and mercy with God that is burden-free. I can have relationship with God because of Jesus, not my performance. I'm loved, blessed, and accepted based on my faith in the cross and not any works of the law. This is what Jesus meant in Matthew 11:30, *"...For My yoke is easy and My burden is light."*

LAW WORKS WRATH

One of the biggest revelations I ever received from God was the law, not our sins, worked God's wrath. Romans 4:15 says, *"... because the law brings about wrath; for where there is no law there is no transgression."* It was the law that worked God's wrath, not our sin! That's why He waited so long to give the law. God didn't give the law—a representation of His goodness and standard for living—to Adam, Abel, Enoch, Noah, or Abram because God knew the law would bring wrath on all disobedience. Curses would come with any violation of the law. God's nature is love and mercy. He never wanted to pour out wrath and punishment on people. But He is also righteous and just. He could not allow sin to go unpunished or unrestrained indefinitely. *"For until the law sin was in the world, but sin is not imputed when there is no law. Nevertheless death reigned from Adam to Moses"* (Rom. 5:13-14). Even though God was longsuffering and patient, even though He wasn't holding sin against us before the law, sin still brought death to all. Sin has consequences. It destroys everything it touches whether God pours out wrath for it or not. Sin harms us, others, and God's good creation. Sin gives Satan place to steal, kill, and destroy (Rom. 6:16 / John 10:10).

When Adam sinned, God did not reveal the full weight of his sin to Adam and Eve. It would have destroyed their relationship. Instead, He was merciful to them. Adam and Eve experienced the consequences of their sin, as we all do, but they did not experience wrath for what they unleashed on humanity. Wrath would have pushed them into despair. It would have left no hope of recovery.

Sin has consequences. It destroys everything it touches whether God pours out wrath for it or not.

The same was true of Cain. When Cain killed his brother, Abel, Cain felt those consequences. But God was merciful. Cain did not experience God's wrath for murder that was revealed under the law as a capital offense. God did not even curse Cain. The ground cursed Cain (see Gen. 4:11). Every time Cain tried to work the ground or plant seed, the ground remembered the innocent blood he spilt, and it refused to produce anything but weeds and thorns for him. God was merciful and put a mark on him to protect him from vengeful assaults by others. God said, *"Whosoever slayeth Cain, vengeance shall be taken on him sevenfold. And the Lord set a mark upon Cain, lest any finding him should kill him"* (Gen. 4:15 KJV).

God was merciful and loving toward humanity, but humanity did not respond to God's love. Then, in the days of Noah, with only eight righteous people left on the whole earth, God continued to reach out for relationship. Think about that. If God wanted to pour out wrath, why wait until there were only eight righteous people left on the whole earth? God loved humanity unconditionally. He was merciful and kind, but sin was wiping out the human race. Noah and his family were the only ones in the whole world who loved God and tried to follow His leading. To save those few and the rest of creation from the effects of sin, God cleansed the earth with a flood. He started over with eight people and all the animals onboard the ark.

Unfortunately, in our fallen condition, we humans could not help but sin. We could not help but wallow in selfishness and pride. And Satan took advantage of it, stealing, killing, and destroying until God finally had to send the law (see John 10:10). The law was given to put a restraint on sin and Satan. God could have flooded the earth a hundred more times, and it would not have changed the heart of man.

> *As by one man sin entered into the world, and death by sin; and so death passed upon all men, for that all have sinned. (For until the law sin was in the world: but sin is not imputed when there is no law.)*
>
> **Romans 5:12-13 (KJV)**

Sin was in the world before the law, but God was not holding sin against the sinner. However, the consequence of sin was bringing death to all humankind (see Rom. 6:23). Sin hardens the human heart. It deadens the conscience, and we, under Satan's rule, will destroy ourselves and others in time (see Heb. 3:13). The law put a restraint on sin until God could get Jesus in the earth to save us from ourselves. Jesus came and changed our hearts. He destroyed Satan's power so we could overcome sin and defend ourselves against Satan's schemes. The law couldn't change the human heart. It couldn't make us righteous (see Gal. 2:21). But it could make us aware of our own failings and keep us from yielding to Satan. The law was a temporary measure added to the Abrahamic covenant. Like a parent or guardian, it protected and corrected us until Jesus could come. And like *"a schoolmaster,"* it drove us to faith in Christ (Gal. 3:24-25 KJV). But once we came to Christ and received Him by faith, we no longer needed the law. It had served its purpose (see Gal. 3:19).

The law put a restraint on sin until God could get Jesus in the earth to save us from ourselves. Jesus came and changed our hearts.

LAW REVEALS SIN

The law had a purpose, but that purpose was not to make us righteous or reveal God. After thousands of years of human history engulfed in sin, we needed something to help us see that we could not be righteous by ourselves. We needed the law to show us how we had missed God's mark, His standard of glory and goodness (see Rom. 3:23). *"Therefore by the deeds of the law no flesh will be justified in his sight, for by the law is the* ***knowledge of sin***" (Rom. 3:20). The law wasn't given to justify us. It wasn't given to make us righteous. The law revealed sin. It showed us how unrighteous we truly were and kept us from comparing ourselves to others so we could be saved by faith (see Rom. 7:7; 1 Cor. 15:56). For who wants to be the best sinner ever to go to hell (see 2 Cor. 10:12)? The law reveals how all of us have sinned and come short of God's glory (Rom. 3:23). The law stopped our mouths. It shut us up before God and revealed our need for Jesus (see Rom. 3:19). It revealed our guilt and sin, driving us to faith in Christ to be saved from our sin. It revealed how unrighteous we were so we would put faith in Christ to be made righteous by faith.

Now, when we come to Christ in our initial act of repentance, we recognize our sin under the law and turn to God for salvation apart from the law. We accept God's love and forgiveness by believing in Jesus and confessing Him as Lord (see Rom. 10:9-10). And everything is made new (see 2 Cor. 5:17). We are perfected forever in our born-again spirit, but it takes grace and time for our natural life to reflect that change (see Heb. 10:14).

What many believers fail to recognize is that every bit of change that comes into our lives comes from repentance. To repent means to change your mind and direction. It is an act of faith—an acknowledgment that God's way is better than our own and a decision to leave our way to follow God's. Unfortunately, most believers don't see change because they don't see the power of repentance. They quit changing their minds to align with God's ways. We must keep coming to Jesus in the renewing of our minds which is a form of repentance. Many are simply married to the philosophies, thoughts, and ways of this world instead of married to Jesus and His thoughts and ways. To be yoked up to Jesus is to be renewed in our minds.

A recent survey showed that 83 percent of Americans claim to be Christians. But if that were so, how could our country be in the mess it's in? If God's ways were dominating the 83 percent, we would see different voting results and different business and entertainment outcomes. We would not allow our children to be taught sexual perversion. We would not allow marriage to be undermined and redefined. We would not promote identity confusion or racism, and lies would not dominate the six o'clock news. Now I'm not saying all those people aren't born again. But they have ceased to repent. God's Word isn't affecting their attitudes. It's not changing the way they think or live.

To be yoked up to Jesus is to be renewed in our minds.

John the Baptist warned the Pharisees to flee a day of wrath to come and, *"Prove by the way you live that you have repented of your sins and turned to God"* (Matt. 3:8 NLT). Are those who claim to be Christians proving they have repented of their sins by the way they live? Have they taken His yoke upon them?

> *Therefore we also, since we are surrounded by so great a cloud of witnesses, let us lay aside every*

> *weight, and the sin which so easily ensnares us, and let us run with endurance the race that is set before us, looking unto Jesus, the author and finisher of our faith, who for the joy that was set before Him endured the cross, despising the shame, and has sat down at the right hand of the throne of God.*
>
> **Hebrews 12:1-2**

Paul instructed us to *"lay aside every weight,"* whether that be sin, habits, or even good things that distract us from Christ, so we can run our race of faith. And while your weights may differ from mine, all of us are tempted to become yoked to something besides Jesus. Some look to Moses and the law to please God and live holy. Others look to themselves, relying on their willpower, to overcome trials and temptations. Many today are married to their politics and refuse to let God's Word come between them and how they think or believe. Their loyalty to Jesus pales in comparison to their political party. But Jesus, the Author and Finisher of our faith, calls us to "*look unto Him.*"

If you're carrying a weight of legalism, leave that religion and cleave to Jesus. Religion will wear you out, push you down, and mess you up. Jesus offers you rest. Get married to Jesus and divorce all those rules and regulations for justification and righteousness with God. Jesus did what you couldn't do—He kept the law—to pay for what you did do—you broke the law—so that you could experience relationship with God—apart from the law. Let Jesus be your hero Husband, your covenant Partner (see 2 Cor. 11:2). Take His yoke upon you and let Him lead you through the challenges of life, being careful not to return to the yoke of the law or any other yokes in our society.

Galatians 5:1 says, *"Stand fast therefore in the liberty by which Christ has made us free, and do not be entangled again with a* ***yoke of bondage****."* This verse is a direct reference to the law of Moses. Here, Paul said the law was a "yoke of bondage" no matter when or why we came to it. But Jesus' yoke is "easy and light" (see Matt. 11:30). Jesus fulfilled every requirement of the law. He took on that weight so that He could offer us a yoke of liberty and freedom (see 2 Cor. 3:17). This new liberty allows us to run to God not from Him in any failure. In my marriage relationship with Jesus, divorce is not an option. He will never leave or forsake me (Heb. 13:5). It is grace that makes this liberty possible.

Grace breaks the power of sin in our lives. It frees us from guilt, shame, and condemnation by freeing us from the burden of the law. The law points to us. It exposes our efforts of self-righteousness and amplifies our guilt when we fail to uphold God's righteous standard. And while guilt can be a good thing if it leads to repentance, it can morph into shame if we don't purge it from our consciences by the blood of Jesus (see Heb. 9:14). (Later, I will deal with this in more detail, but for now, I want to say guilt is sorrow over a committed sin. Shame believes that sin is now part of the identity of the sinner.) Romans 5:20 declares, *"Moreover the law entered that the offense might abound. But where sin*

In my marriage relationship with Jesus, divorce is not an option.

abounded, grace abounded much more." Sin—and the guilt, condemnation, and fear it produces—enslaves the masses. But God's grace is greater. It destroys the tyranny of sin and offers liberty to all who will yoke up to Jesus and receive His grace through faith (see Eph. 2:8).

> *If we confess our sins, He is faithful and just to forgive us our sins and to cleanse us from all unrighteousness.*
>
> **1 John 1:9**

Often, the first question people have when they hear this message is, "If God has made me righteous by grace, why do I have to keep repenting?" Repentance is something we'll be doing for the rest of our lives. I repent and believe to become part of God's Kingdom, and I keep on repenting as I learn to change my mind and walk in His ways. I see things totally different than I did ten years ago. And that change has come through repentance. It's not automatic. I have to agree with God and choose to mix faith with His Word to open the floodgates of the Kingdom in my life. Every time I choose to meditate on God and His Word and change my mind and direction, I open that gate. Every time I choose to meditate on lies or the philosophies of this world or my old way of thinking, I close that gate and experience fear. I haven't lost my salvation. I'm still God's child and part of His Kingdom, but I don't see the benefits of that Kingdom until I change my mind.

Repentance is the heart of the gospel. Jesus preached, *"Repent of your sins and turn to God, for the Kingdom of*

Heaven is near" (Matt. 4:17 NLT). And later, *"The time promised by God has come at last!' He announced 'The kingdom of God is near! Repent of your sins and believe the Good News!'"* (Mark 1:15 NLT). John the Baptist preached the same message. So did Peter. On the Day of Pentecost, Peter told the crowds they had killed their promised Messiah but God raised Him from the dead. This Jesus, he said, was both Lord and Messiah, and He offered salvation to the whole world. Acts 2:37-38 says,

> *Now when they heard this, they were cut to the heart, and said to Peter and the rest of the apostles, "Men and brethren, what shall we do?" then Peter said to them, "**Repent**, and let every one of you be baptized in the name of Jesus Christ for the remission of sins."*

"The Kingdom of heaven is here," they preached. "Don't condone, defend, justify, or glorify sin. Repent—change your mind—and turn to God. That's the only way into God's Kingdom." But repentance is not the same as remorse. If you've raised kids, you know that. Think of a time when your child disobeyed. Though they may have started crying as you corrected them, it might not have been because they were sorry. It could have just been the embarrassment of getting caught. They were sorrowful but not repentant. Repentance is a change of mind and direction. Though some Christians believe you only need to repent of sin once when entering God's Kingdom and giving your life to Christ, how many of us have done something stupid or thought something wrong since being born again? How many times have we needed to change our minds or direction? Recognizing that need and

Repentance is a change of mind and direction.

seeking God's grace to empower that change is repentance. It's not necessary that we are "born again" again every time we mess up. But we do need to repent (see 1 John 1:9).

Now I have to be careful here. For there are also Christians, like those in the group I came out of, who believe, if you don't "repent" twenty times a day, you aren't sincere and may not be saved. They think repentance is "throwing yourself on God's mercy" as you cry, bawl, and wail over sin. But remember, remorse is not necessarily repentance. It depends on how we respond to sin. When we truly see sin from God's perspective and ourselves in light of His love, we will experience a godly sorrow over sin. We will be sincerely sorry for what sin has done to our families and communities, and for the role we played in death by cooperating with sin. But that type of sorrow leads to repentance. It is not condemning. It does not produce uncertainty. Second Corinthians 7:10 says, *"Godly sorrow produces repentance."* Godly sorrow always results in a change of mind. And in time, that change will affect the way you live your life as long as you stay yoked up to Jesus. After His resurrection, Jesus called five out of the seven churches listed in the book of Revelation to repent. Only two of them were on the right course of God's will for them as a light in their cities (Smyrna and Philadelphia) (see Rev. 2:8 & 3:7). The other five were told to repent. The consequences of their lack of repentance (changing their mind and direction) would lead to the removal of their lampstand—their church in the city (see Rev. 2:5). This was just one of the many consequences of not repenting. These people did not need to repent to get saved, they had already done that. They had gotten "off track" and needed to get back on track to accomplish their assignment in the city. How do they do that? Repent!

So, if you sin, repent quickly and receive God's mercy and forgiveness. Unload that guilt onto Jesus so you can overcome condemnation by His grace. Reverse the consequences or wages of sin by changing your mind and direction. God's mercies *"are new every morning"* (Lam. 3:22-23). He doesn't condemn us. Our consciences do that. God's attitude toward us, even when we fail, is mercy. The Word promises, *"I will be merciful to their unrighteousness, and their sins and iniquities will I remember no more"* (Heb. 8:12).

He doesn't condemn us. Our consciences do that. God's attitude toward us, even when we fail, is mercy.

"What about God's chastisement?" God does chasten, or correct, us as children. But He does so in love not wrath (see Heb. 12:5-6). And John wrote, *"If our heart condemns us, God is greater than our heart, and knows all things"* (1 John 3:20). What are the *"things"* God knows that our hearts may not? How complete our forgiveness and acceptance are because of grace! Never doubt God's love for you. Never doubt how complete your forgiveness is. You may not understand how loved and forgiven you are, but God does! Take His yoke upon you and receive of His mercy and grace.

Chapter Three

DIMENSIONS OF GRACE

As each one has received a gift, minister it to one another, as good stewards of the manifold grace of God.

1 Peter 4:10

The grace of God can be a difficult concept to grasp and not for a lack of good teaching. There is an emergence of grace happening within the Body of Christ right now, and it's exciting. Grace is difficult to grasp because it's what the apostle Peter called *"manifold." Manifold* means many-sided. Like a diamond, other Bible translations call grace *"multifaceted"* (AMP) or even a *"many-colored tapestry"* (TPT). God's grace is more than what we say before consuming our food. It's also more than the common definition of "unmerited favor" (though it certainly involves favor we did not earn). Grace is also the power to change. And according to the Amplified Classic translation of 1 Peter 4:10, grace is the *"...diverse powers and gifts granted to Christians."* It is certainly a "manifold" grace! But many within the Body of Christ struggle to balance the theology of grace with its practical application. We are all growing in our knowing of God's grace in our lives.

The third rhythm of grace is found in Matthew 11:29 (KJV), *"learn of me."* Grace is a vital part of the revelation that comes from Jesus Himself. Paul told young Timothy in 2 Timothy 2:1 to *"be strong in the grace that is in Christ Jesus."* We discover and find grace in Jesus by revelation.

There are two primary dimensions of grace. (God's grace is multifaceted. But for teaching purposes, each aspect of His grace can be categorized into this larger framework.) One dimension is simply an understanding of what grace is—the theology of grace. The other dimension is an understanding of what grace does—its application. So, grace *is* something, and grace *does* something. Grace is God's unmerited favor in your life. It is God abounding toward you in favor, blessing, love, and goodness. But many believers camp out on this theological dimension of grace and miss its power. And though this definition is not incorrect, it is incomplete. Titus 2:11–12 (KJV) says:

We discover and find grace in Jesus by revelation.

> *For the grace of God that bringeth salvation hath appeared to all men,* ***teaching us that****, denying ungodliness and worldly lusts, we should live soberly, righteously, and godly, in this present world.*

Grace is our change-agent. Grace is God's unmerited favor that brings salvation and every other good thing in Christ. And grace teaches us to live and serve God amid a crooked and perverse generation. It doesn't release us for unholy living.

We've all heard "grace covers sin." That is nowhere in scripture. Love covers sin (1 Pet. 4:8 / Prov. 10:12). Grace empowers and teaches us how to overcome sin. Even under grace, sin is still deadly. But the good news of grace is not that God ignores your sin. The good news is that Jesus has provided the way back to God in spite of your sin. He has ransomed you out of sin's grasp, out of its tyranny. Now, instead of being dominated by sin or by your flesh, you can experience the kind of life God always intended for you to live—a Kingdom-life (see Rom. 6:22; 8:9). You don't have to carry around the pain and guilt of sin (see Rom. 5:20; 6:14). You can be dominated by grace. All you have to do is believe—respond to His grace by faith (see Rom. 3:22-24). And though this new way of living can take time to learn, like a good father, God is patient with us as we cooperate with His grace and walk by faith. Grace empowers us to overcome every situation we face as we look to God. It brings about a new level of "being in Christ" and "doing in life." Grace is the only way to overcome sin, Satan, and the fear and worry we experience in this world. It is the only way we can be truly free (see Rom. 8:1-3; Gal. 5:1).

Grace is what empowered Paul to become a new creation and do the works of an apostle. In 1 Corinthians 15:10, Paul said, *"But by the grace of God* ***I am what I am,*** *and His grace toward me was not in vain; but I* ***labored*** *more abundantly than they all, yet not I, but the* ***grace of God*** *which was with me."* Grace is God's power to be and to do. It is what empowers us to be new creations and do the works of Jesus. It makes us righteous before God, empowering us to live godly lives. Grace made Paul an apostle and it was grace that empowered him to do the work of one. In grace, God saves, changes, and empowers us to live lives that please Him and bring Him glory.

At nine years old, I had an encounter with God I didn't know how to explain. But I knew He had called me to preach, so I packed a bag and headed out the door. Of course, I had no idea at nine how to discern this call of grace or what to do with it. I thought grace was something you said before a meal. It wasn't until I rededicated my life to Christ in 1980 and immersed myself in the Word of God that I began to understand how the grace of God could empower me to be who He called me to be and do what He called me to do. You can't just decide to be a pastor or evangelist or any other ministry gift in the Body. Those things take grace. And if you don't know how to receive that grace-gift from Jesus, you will fail and could ultimately damage yourself, your family, and others. I have a grace from Jesus to teach His Word—in both written and spoken formats. Not everyone has been given that grace. But that doesn't mean you don't have a God-given gift of grace. Your grace-gift may be to sing or work with kids. Whatever you've been called to be and do within the Kingdom, there is a grace there to accomplish that call. It is a part of His manifold grace.

Whatever you've been called to be and do within the Kingdom, there is a grace there to accomplish that call. It is a part of His manifold grace.

When we distance ourselves from this grace—either through misunderstanding, wrong teaching, or willful disobedience—we cannot help but feel the effects of sin. Guilt, fear, condemnation, worry, anxiety, and stress are all fruits of an overloaded, overcharged heart, a heart set on pride and self-effort. Grace breaks sin's dominion and effect in our lives. It teaches and empowers us to overcome these things through humility. The more we humble ourselves, the more grace can fill our weaknesses.

James 4:6 says, *"But He gives more grace. Therefore He says: 'God resists the proud, but gives grace to the humble.'"* Notice how grace is more than just unmerited favor. We can do something to get more of it—humble ourselves. Admit and submit our weaknesses to God. Acknowledge our need for God's power and strength to overcome sin. Look to God versus self (pride). We need grace to stop doing wrong things and grace to do the right things. No wonder we call it "amazing grace." In 2 Corinthians 12:7, Paul mentioned a messenger sent by Satan *"to buffet"* and discourage him in ministry. According to *Strong's Concordance, buffet* is to "rap with the fist" or beat repeatedly (*kolaphizo,* G2852). Imagine waves on a beach that come in repeatedly and beat or buffet the shore. Satan was opposing Paul like that. Through afflictions, persecutions, and heavy tribulation, Satan was trying to silence Paul and discourage others from following Paul's example. While people saw great power in his life; they also saw great persecution and hardship. Paul sought the Lord for relief three times, and God's response was always, *"My grace is sufficient for you, for My strength is made perfect in weakness"* (2 Cor. 12:9).

Wow! Grace is God's strength in human weakness. That's why we get more grace in humility and forfeit grace in pride. Pride is all about self-sufficiency. It is independence from God.

Paul came to Jesus three times. And despite what he faced, he remained yoked to Him and learned to:

> *...take pleasure in infirmities, in reproaches, in needs, in persecutions, in distresses, for Christ's sake. For when I am weak, then I am strong.*
>
> **2 Corinthians 12:10**

God's power and strength works in our weakness (humility), not our strength after the flesh (pride). After coming to Jesus and yoking up to Him, it is imperative that we also develop the rhythm of learning of Him (see Matt. 11:29). No matter what situation you or I face, or what you may be going through right now, God wants to reveal Himself to you. He wants you to recognize that His presence is with you. And He wants you to learn of Him in every circumstance. All of us go through problems. Each of us has issues. We're all bombarded by things that try to overwhelm our hearts and take us away from God. But instead of stressing out when you face problems, instead of worrying about how to get out of your problems, learn to find God in them. Keep growing in knowing God.

God's power and strength works in our weakness (humility), not our strength after the flesh (pride).

Paul referred to this concept again in Philippians when he said,

> *Be anxious for nothing, but in everything by prayer and supplication, with thanksgiving, let your requests be made known to God; and the peace of God, which surpasses all understanding, will guard your hearts and minds through Christ Jesus.*
>
> **Philippians 4:6-7**

Instead of worrying about the future or being anxious about the past, we are to "come to Jesus" in prayer. There, in His presence, we unload our hearts and become yoked to Him rather than our problems. We experience His supernatural peace and learn to rest in Him so that we can recover from all those feelings of overwhelm.

Peter said it this way in 1 Peter 5:6-7: "Therefore humble yourselves under the mighty hand of God, that He may exalt you in due time, casting all your care upon Him, for He cares for you." Notice that unloading our care upon the Lord requires humility. It is not an act of irresponsibility but rather of partnership. It requires faith—faith that He truly cares for us and will take care of us. And faith that as believers we are not alone in anything we face.

When our church caught fire in June of 2002, I would have been filled with worry and fear had I not known what I'm sharing with you right now. That fear could have easily destroyed me, my family, and our congregation, but as I stood in the parking lot watching the church burn, I told the Lord, "You have a problem."

People may laugh at me for that, but they simply don't understand. In that moment, I knew I had to give that

As I stood in the parking lot watching the church burn, I told the Lord, "You have a problem."

problem to God. I had to trust His grace. I couldn't carry the weight of rebuilding the church or let worry get into my heart. So, I prayed: "Lord, You said, *'I will build My church, and the gates of* [hell] *shall not prevail against it'* (Matt. 16:18). I'm just an under-shepherd here. I'll facilitate whatever You direct me to do in faith, but this is not my problem. It's Yours, and I'm not going to leave You while You're going through this problem." That may sound strange as well, but it was simply my voice of faith reversing even the thought of Him leaving me right in the middle of trouble. If I wasn't willing to leave Him, He certainly would never leave me!

And God proved Himself faithful. His grace was sufficient in our human weakness. He gave us the strength and wisdom to rebuild that building bigger and better than before. And He built that church into a multi-site congregation that is still growing and affecting the surrounding communities today.

That's what casting our care on the Lord is all about. It's learning to keep worry and fear out of our hearts by unloading it onto God as an act of faith and humility. Many feel that God leaves them in trials and tribulation. They think they must carry the problem and come up with solutions on their own. That is not true. Dear ones, we can trust God with our problems. Don't try to shoulder a weight you were not meant to carry. You'll only collapse and may even end up blaming God for something He didn't do. Talk to God. Cast your care on Him and guard your heart from worry. Trust Him to engage with you in grace. Keep coming to Jesus. Stay yoked up to Him and learn of Him. These three rhythms of grace point us toward intimacy with our Savior. They bring us back *"to the throne of grace"* so we can find the grace we need for every issue we face (Heb. 4:16).

In January of 2020, I had a heart issue that required bypass surgery (five to be exact). It was a scary time for my wife and family, but Sue still reflects on the presence of God that was with her in a nearly tangible way as she faced tough decisions and many unknowns after we arrived at the emergency room (ER). (Most people want to hear my testimony from this fiery trial. They want to know about my death experience and the conversation I had with Jesus. They want to hear about heaven. And while all that is good, Sue's perspective really blesses me.) Sue had to stand and fight the good fight of faith when her senses were screaming at her to fear. She told me she knew immediately that the attack on my body was an attack of the enemy. She prayed in the Spirit all the way to the hospital and acknowledges how that gave her strength for the battle ahead. By the time we arrived at the ER, she had her armor on and was ready to fight whatever obstacle, circumstance, or negative thought came our way.

For example, she recalls an instance in the ER where I looked at her and said, "Tell the kids I love them." Immediately, she heard the Holy Spirit say to her, "He will have a choice, but he will make the right choice." She understood this was a fight for my life, but she had a promise to stand on, "He will make the right choice." She knew I would experience death but I would choose to come back.

On another occasion, one of the nurses working on me said, "Pastor Duane, do you believe God uses people like us to help?" The answer was and is yes, and Sue began praying specifically over the doctors and nurses that God would guide them, give them wisdom, and use them in the healing process. One of my favorite stories she tells is of how God gave her a vision of angels surrounding the operating room, and at least two other people saw the same thing, giving her peace that the angels were surrounding me and protecting me during surgery. I could go on and on with testimonies of the presence of God during this ordeal but will save it for another time. I'm so thankful for a wife who listens to the Holy Spirit because it took both of us focusing on the Lord, acknowledging His promises, and standing on His Word to fight fear and see the victory. We continue to walk in that victory every single day and thank God for it! Had it not been for the rhythms of grace I'm talking about, I would not be writing this best seller today. (I believe I receive!)

Jesus was and is our continual source of grace. Fear and stress cannot abide at the throne where Jesus sits and we tarry. Again, Second Timothy 2:1 says, *"You therefore, my son, be strong in the grace that is in Christ Jesus."* When we come to Jesus—when we come to grace—and take His yoke upon us and learn of Him, we find the strength to endure and prevail over the trials, afflictions, and adversities of life. God's amazing grace teaches us

Jesus was and is our continual source of grace. Fear and stress cannot abide at the throne where Jesus sits and we tarry.

who we are in Christ. And it teaches us what we can now do through Christ. When we come unto Jesus, we come to grace in all its dimensions. Through simple relationship with Him, Jesus fills our hearts with faith. We respond by casting our care on Him. We lay aside the things that weigh us down and the sin that keeps us from running our race with joy. And He helps us unload the stress, worry, and fear that come from a heart fixed on temporal issues. We overcome the world, and He gives us rest and peace.

Chapter Four

NOT GUILTY

"For I know the plans I have for you," declares the Lord, "plans to prosper you and ***not to harm you***, plans to give you hope and a future."

Jeremiah 29:11 (NIV)

Finding God in our problems does not make Him the author of them. God knows the plans He has for you, and they are all good! But many of us don't have the same confidence in His plans as He does. God does not cause problems. But He is the answer to them. Hebrews 13:5 tells us that God never leaves us or forsakes us. He is with you wherever you go and whatever you face. And while we've all felt confused, disappointed, or burdened while facing problems (me included), that only happens because we're allowing the problem to overwhelm our hearts instead of seeking the One who holds the answer. Thankfully, His grace is sufficient for us even in this as well.

In 1 Corinthians 10:6, we read that everything that happened to Israel was recorded for our admonition and learning. They were for our example: a warning against unbelief. In this letter, Paul also dealt with big issues like idolatry and sexual immorality. He admonished not to tempt the Lord as Israel did and recounted the dangers of murmuring and complaining (1 Cor. 10:9-10). I used to think that murmuring and complaining was no big deal. Everyone I knew early in life murmured and complained. Israel's murmuring and complaining was a manifestation of their unbelief. Hebrews 11:6 tells us that faith pleases God. And thankfulness is the sound of faith. Murmuring and complaining are the sounds of unbelief.

Romans 1:21 says that not being thankful is the first step toward a reprobate mind: *"Although they knew God, they did not glorify Him as God, nor were **thankful**, but became futile in their thoughts, and their foolish hearts were darkened."* Few consider the deadliness of an ungrateful, unthankful heart. And while we are no longer under the law and its curses, murmuring and complaining still displease God because they are not of faith (see Heb. 11:6).

Then, seemingly out of nowhere, Paul talked about the trials we all face in life. He said:

> *There hath no temptation taken you but such as is common to man: but God is faithful....*
>
> 1 Corinthians 10:13 (KJV)

Before we continue, I want you to notice how this verse describes God. He is faithful, not guilty. Whatever hardship, trial, tribulation, or affliction you're going through, God is not guilty. He neither caused it nor willed it. But He is faithful to you in the midst of it. Verse 13 (KJV) concludes:

> ***God is faithful****; who will not suffer you to be tempted above that ye are able; but will with the temptation also make a way to escape, that ye may be able to bear it.*

God's faithfulness to us in suffering is grace. And that grace mixed with our faith produces endurance in our lives. The New Living Translation of this verse begins, "*The temptations in your life are no different from what others experience.*" The devil always wants us to believe that we are an exception to the rule. That no one has ever experienced what we are walking through. That no one understands. That God's promises could not apply to us. That our circumstances are too big, too hard, or lasting too long; we'll never find a way out. Brothers and sisters, this is simply not true.

God's faithfulness to us in suffering is grace.

Early in ministry, I thought the problems I experienced both personally and with the people I was ministering to were unique. I thought nobody had known the trouble I'd seen. Nobody had been shot at and criticized like me. I learned differently and, by the grace of God, have outgrown this belief, but it took a while for me to realize that no matter what I faced someone, somewhere had experienced it too. And just like God was faithful to them and rescued them out of trouble, He would be faithful to me.

Part of living a stress-free life is to stop assuming that your situation is unique and to remember that everything in life is seasonal. You're not going to be in that situation forever.

The devil may try to convince you otherwise, but remember this verse: *"God is faithful. He will not allow the temptation to be more than you can stand. When you are tempted, he will show you a way out so that you can endure"* (1 Cor. 10:13 NLT).

Yet how many people misunderstand God's nature and the word Paul used for *temptation* in 1 Corinthians 10:13? It is the Greek word *peirasmos,* which means proving by "experiment, experience, solicitation, discipline, or provocation" (G3986). Its usage often implies adversity, but it doesn't have to mean that. Its root word *peira* actually means to test, like an assayer tests the quality of gold. God does not put hardship on you. He is not the one tempting you more (or less) than you can bear. He does not dump poverty or sickness or any bad thing on you. He is not overloading your heart or life. God is faithful to you. He is your answer. Your Deliverer. He is your way of escape. However, tests reveal the quality or strength of our faith. And when we rely on God's grace during trials, we develop endurance and are approved before God as the real deal. This knowledge helps us remain joyful and thankful in all circumstances (Rom. 5:3-5; James 1:2-5). We are not just "fair weather" friends of God, but truly love Him regardless of what tries to separate us. A faith that is not tested is not a Bible faith.

I cannot tell you the number of times I've heard this verse shared incorrectly. People say, "God won't give you more than you can handle. He won't put more on you than you can bear," meaning God limits the amount of hardship He brings your way or asks you to endure. But that is not what this verse says. God doesn't put *any* amount of hardship on you. Psalm 34:19 says, *"Many are the afflictions of the righteous, but the Lord*

delivers him out of them all." And James added, *"Let no man say when he is tempted, I am tempted of God: for God cannot be tempted with evil, neither tempteth he any man"* (James 1:13 KJV). How simple is that? But just to make sure you don't miss his point, James went on to say, *"Do not be deceived, my beloved brethren. Every good gift and every perfect gift is from above, and comes down from the Father of lights, with Him there is no variation or shadow of turning"* (James 1:16-17). God is not doing bad things today and good tomorrow! He wills and plans nothing but good for you.

Many Christians are deceived into believing that God tempts them or brings hardship into their lives to teach them. The mistake I made (and that many others make) was to think the Old Testament law revealed God's nature. All the curses, wrath, and even punishment revealed under the law for sin was to teach Israel something. They were curses, not blessings in disguise. It was wrath, not chastening. Jesus delivered us from God's wrath and curses of the law (Rom. 5:9; Gal. 3:13; 1 Thess. 1:10). Even the disciples, at one time, thought God wanted to pour wrath out on people. When Jesus was headed for Jerusalem, He passed through a Samaritan village that did not receive Him. And when His disciples saw it, they said, *"Lord, do You want us to command fire to come down from heaven and consume them, just as Elijah did?"* (Luke 9:54). They thought to emulate an Old Testament prophet who brought judgment on an entire village for not believing (see 2 Kings 1:9-16). But Jesus rebuked them, *"You do not know what manner of spirit you are of. For the Son of Man did not come to destroy men's lives but to save them"* (Luke 9:55-56). Like the Pharisees, the disciples thought God's nature was to punish, not save. They didn't realize that

All the curses, wrath, and even punishment revealed under the law for sin was to teach Israel something. They were curses, not blessings in disguise. It was wrath, not chastening.

while God has wrath, He is love. God's plan is to save us, heal us, bless us, and do us good and not harm. He means absolutely no ill-will toward you. While what Elijah did wasn't sin, it wasn't God's best. We have a better covenant established on better promises (see Heb 8:6).

That's why many in the Body of Christ fear God with a tormenting fear. They falsely accuse Him or blame Him for the problems in their lives. They think He is the author of their trials and hardships. They read the wrath and curses of the law, and knowing their sin, believe their suffering is God justly punishing them for sin. They blame Him for their troubles, but He is not guilty! Wrath is not His blessing in disguise. He is not the one making them sick, poor, and afflicted to bring them back to Himself or teach them a lesson. His plan for us is nothing but good. While God teaches us in all things if we humble ourselves and listen, it doesn't mean He does bad things to teach us. If one of my children was backed into by a car, I would teach them that cars can harm or kill them; however, I would never back into them with a car to teach them how deadly cars can be. You would have me arrested for child abuse, yet we accuse God of no less.

JESUS REVEALS GOD

God's true nature is only revealed in grace—in Jesus. And grace inspires a healthy, reverential fear—an attitude of respect and honor, an awe-inspiring worship—of God. This is the true "fear of the Lord." Grace helps us recognize the blessings, riches, and long life that our loving Father gives His greatest treasure.

> *For the law was given through Moses, but grace and truth came through Jesus Christ.*
>
> John 1:17

Moses (the law) was given to reveal sin (see Rom 3:20). Jesus (the embodiment of grace and truth) came to reveal God (see Heb. 1:3). John 1:14 says, *"And the Word became flesh and dwelt among us, and we **beheld His glory**, the glory as of the only begotten of the Father, full of grace and truth."* If you wonder what God looks like, sounds like, or acts like, look to Jesus. Jesus didn't make anyone sick or call fire down on anyone. He *"went about doing good and healing all who were oppressed by the devil"* (Acts 10:38). The Pharisees thought God's nature was angry, wrathful, and vengeful. Yet, Jesus, who claimed to be God's Son, did none of those things. That's part of why they missed Him. They were looking for something other than what He was.

> *He is the **image** of the invisible God, the firstborn over all creation.*
>
> Colossians 1:15

If you wonder what God looks like, sounds like, or acts like, look to Jesus.

*If you had known Me, you would have known My Father also; and from now on you know Him and have **seen Him.***

John 14:7

*Philip said to Him, "Lord, show us the Father, and it is sufficient for us." Jesus said to him, "Have I been with you so long, and yet you have not known Me, Philip? He who has **seen Me** has **seen the Father**; so how can you say, 'Show us the Father'?"*

John 14:8-9

*Who being the brightness of His glory and **the express image** of His person, and upholding all things by the word of His power, when He had by Himself purged our sins, sat down at the right hand of the Majesty on high.*

Hebrews 1:3

Jesus is God's selfie! He is the visible image of an invisible God. He is God made flesh—an exact representation of His Being. If you have seen Jesus, you have seen the Father. Jesus didn't come to reveal a side of God. He didn't reveal just part of God. He revealed the fullness of God. *"For in Him dwells all the fullness of the Godhead bodily"* (Col. 2:9). And while He warned of a day of wrath to come for the disobedient and unbelieving, He never cursed anyone. Jesus came to save us *"from the wrath to come"* (Rom. 5:8-10; 1 Thess. 1:10).

Jesus is God's selfie!

There is so much misunderstanding between Old Testament law and New Testament grace. To see the law in capsule form, I encourage you to read Deuteronomy 28:15-68. It outlines the terrible curses for disobedience under the law. Under the law, God was the One who struck the people with a plague after complaining about the food He provided (see Num. 11). God struck Miriam with leprosy when she dishonored Moses and questioned his authority (see Num. 12). God opened the ground and swallowed Korah and all who rebelled with him (see Num. 16). And God sent serpents among the children of Israel when they grew impatient with God's promise and spoke rashly (see Num. 21:4-9). Those punishments were not God's blessings in disguise. They weren't teaching tools. They were curses. Period. This subject is worthy of its own book, but under New Testament grace, we can be confident that:

> *Christ hath redeemed us from the* ***curse of the law****, being made a curse for us: for it is written, Cursed is everyone that hangeth on a tree: that the blessing of Abraham might come on the Gentiles through Jesus Christ; that we might receive the promise of the Spirit through faith.*
>
> Galatians 3:13-14 (KJV)

God is not punishing us today. Jesus bore the punishment—the curses—for our sins on the cross. We've been redeemed from all Old Testament curses and are justified by faith so that we can receive the blessing of Abraham.

> *There is therefore now* ***no condemnation*** *to those who are in Christ Jesus, who do not walk according to the flesh, but according to the Spirit. For the law of the Spirit of life in Christ Jesus has made me free from the law of sin and death. For what the law could not do in that it was weak through the flesh, God did by sending His own Son in the likeness of sinful flesh, on account of sin: He condemned sin in the flesh, that the righteous requirement of the law might be fulfilled in us who do not walk according to the flesh but according to the Spirit.*
>
> Romans 8:1-4

God is not condemning us. He poured wrath on Jesus for our sake. Jesus bore all sickness, all poverty, all depression, all addiction, and all lack on the cross. This is the gospel of grace. God is not mad at you. He is not repaying you for what your sins deserve. He's not even keeping track. God condemned sin in Jesus' flesh so that we could be abundantly blessed. He proved His love for you at the cross and made peace with humanity (see Col. 1:20). God is not against you. He is not guilty of harming you or your family, no matter what the ignorant and unlearned claim. God is for you. And *"if God is"* for you, *"who can be against"* you (Rom. 8:31)? There is no need to fear. You are His beloved child. And He is your faithful God (see

1 Cor. 10:13). He is not the author of your problems. But He is the way out.

With Him, we can endure and overcome anything that life or Satan throws our way. Isaiah, looking forward to Messiah and the work of the cross, declared:

> *"Do not fear, for you will not be ashamed; neither be disgraced, for you will not be put to shame.... For your Maker is your husband, the Lord of hosts is His name; and your Redeemer is the Holy One of Israel.... But with everlasting kindness I will have mercy on you," says the Lord, your Redeemer.... "For as I have sworn that the waters of Noah would no longer cover the earth, so have I sworn that I would not be* ***angry with you****, nor* ***rebuke you****. For the mountains shall depart and the hills be removed, but My kindness shall not depart from you, nor shall* ***My covenant of peace*** *be removed," says the Lord, who has mercy on you.*
>
> **Isaiah 54:4-5, 8-10**

This is so awesome! God has sworn that He will not be angry with us. His kindness will never be removed. We have a New Covenant, a New Testament, with Him. And it is a covenant of peace, not fear, worry, or anxiety. We should not try to serve God under Old Covenant law. We should not allow fear to undermine our faith. But we should strive to understand this New Testament of grace that reveals His faithfulness in every circumstance. For He promised, this covenant will not

God has sworn that He will not be angry with us. His kindness will never be removed.

be removed. God chastens and corrects us as His children, but it is in love, *not* wrath (see Heb. 12:5-11). Even His rebukes are out of love and care for us.

The grace of God is our "no fear" zone. We can come to Jesus in any trial or affliction and, at His feet, find a yoke of fellowship and relationship that invites us to learn of Him and rejoice over the great salvation we have through Him. Let us not complain or worry about every hardship in our lives as the Israelites did but let us be thankful. Consider 2 Corinthians 2:14 which says, *"Now thanks be to God who always leads us in triumph in Christ, and through us diffuses the fragrance of His knowledge in every place."* Through Jesus—through grace—God always causes us to triumph. He neither causes nor condones the yoke of fear and worry the world throws upon us. Grace has redeemed us from that. And now, today, God wants to reveal Himself—His true self—to you so that the beauty and fragrance of His goodness, love, and faithfulness can be experienced and shared everywhere you go.

Chapter Five

THE POWER OF CHOICE

I call heaven and earth as witness today against you, that I have set before you life and death, blessing and cursing; therefore choose life, that both you and your descendants may live.

Deuteronomy 30:19

Never underestimate the power of choice. In Luke 21, Jesus taught on the challenges of the end times. He spoke of wars and rumors of wars, earthquakes, pestilences (which are viruses), and kingdoms rising against kingdoms. He said there would be persecutions, the saints would be imprisoned, and many false prophets would arise to deceive. But He said, *"By your patience possess your souls"* (Luke 21:19).

Wow! When we see terrible things coming upon the earth or hear about them in the news, we must recognize them for what they are, and with patience, possess our souls. *Possess* means "to harness" or control. It's a word picture that means to rein in your soul like a rider would rein in a horse. We are to control our minds when we hear of these things and not let our emotions or thoughts run wild, taking us captive with their lies. Do not let these things trouble or overwhelm you. In John

14:1, Jesus said, *"Let not your heart be troubled; you believe in God, believe also in Me." "Let"* here means to choose. We can choose to have a trouble-free heart. We cannot choose to have a trouble-free life, but we can choose to have a trouble-free heart.

The truth is we choose to have emotional breakdowns. We choose to fall apart and be discouraged. I know that sounds harsh to someone dealing with those feelings, but part of living and walking by faith is choosing to *"let not your heart be troubled."* I once came home after a long day and told my wife, "I'm going to have a nervous breakdown, and you're not going to stop me! I worked hard for this, and I deserve it." We've all had those days. We *want* to have a fit and give someone—anyone—a piece of our minds. But by letting our emotions control us, we submit to the flesh and choose to have a trouble-filled heart instead of a trouble-free one.

Have you ever noticed that most of the bad decisions you've made in life were made while you were in an emotional state? During those times, stress and fear are more likely to dominate your thoughts and affect how you process information. And you are more likely to have a flesh-flash. A flesh-flash is when you are strictly emotionally driven. The mind of Christ in your spirit man is canceled out, and unwise decisions usually ensue. That's why patience is so important. During these times, we shouldn't try to make important decisions. But neither can we ignore what's happening around us. We must choose to fix our thoughts on God. We must, in patience, possess our souls so that troubled times don't take root in our minds and overwhelm our hearts with fear. It all starts with a choice.

Jesus said that in the last days there would be *"signs in the sun, in the moon, and in the stars"* and that entire nations would experience confusion and distress until *"men's hearts fail*[ed] *them from fear"* (Luke 21:25-26). Fear is deadly. If we let it, fear will overwhelm our hearts and overload our lives. But that's not the only thing Jesus mentioned in this passage that causes the heart to be overwhelmed. Luke 21:26 (KJV) ends with, men *"looking after those things which are coming on the earth."* When we are focused on our circumstances instead of God's faithfulness, we sink just like Peter when he walked on water (see Matt. 14:22-33).

Many people give Peter a hard time. But they forget he walked on water! He did the impossible. It wasn't until he took his eyes off Jesus and saw the wind and waves that he began to sink. (The wind and waves didn't affect his ability to walk on water. You can't stay on top of water when all is calm!) Dear ones, your circumstances are not hindering you from experiencing God's goodness. They are not keeping you from living your "best life." Neither are they responsible for the stress and fear you feel. Anxiety is not caused by what's going on around you. It's caused by what's going on *in* you. Everyone on this planet experiences hard things. Consider Paul. In Acts 22-28, Paul was put on trial for His faith. In chapter 26, he stood before yet another magistrate and King Agrippa after being unjustly imprisoned for two years. After hearing a summary of the case, the king gave Paul permission to defend himself. Most people I know would use that time to have

Fear is deadly. If we let it, fear will overwhelm our hearts and overload our lives.

a pity party in front of a captive audience. They'd rail about the injustice of their situation or complain about how'd they'd been misunderstood and mistreated. Not Paul. He began his defense with, *"I think myself happy..."* (Acts 26:2). Wow! Is that how you'd respond—I think myself happy?

For years, I thought I was either happy or not. I didn't know I had a choice, and I think most of us start there. We're not taught to control our moods. We're not taught that peace and happiness are choices. I hear people say all the time, "I can't help it. I just got up on the wrong side of the bed." If that's the case, you need to figure out which side of the bed is the right side and park the wrong side up against the wall so you can get up on the right side of the bed every day. The choice to control our emotions is not all there is to happiness, but it starts there.

If our feelings weren't a choice, how could Jesus say, *"Let not your heart be troubled"* (John 14:1)? How could He command us to do something we are incapable of? Or how could Paul say, *"I think myself happy,"* while he was in chains? Those responses were not just an automatic, built-in part of their character. They were a choice.

Everyone deals with circumstances they can't control. And everyone has a choice to deal with those circumstances by faith or to yield to fear. Most people believe the opposite is true. They point to everything that's going on in their lives as just cause for being stressed. They say anyone would be stressed if they had to deal with those problems. But I know people who are living life with even more problems, and they aren't stressed, or fear driven. I have more problems today than I've ever had (maybe even more than what you have), but I'm not stressed or driven by fear.

Scripture says that *"faith comes by hearing, and hearing"* God's Word (Rom. 10:17). Fear comes in a similar way. It comes by hearing and hearing the gloom and doom of the world. Fear focuses on the problem, on the negative circumstance. Faith focuses on God's promises and faithfulness. While Paul was on trial, he knew God would turn things around and use his imprisonment for His glory and Kingdom. And we can know the same thing. We don't have to be led through life by our emotions. The things happening around us do not have to create anxiety or fear.

Most people blame circumstances or other people for their problems. They think, "If only they would change." Or, "If I could just get away from this person or that situation everything would be fine." I can't tell you how many times spouses do this to each other. But when they get rid of their spouse, nothing much changes. (Perhaps they're looking at the wrong spouse!) Dear ones, your spouse, your kids, and your family are not your problem. Neither is your boss or coworker. As a believer, the problems you're dealing with do not have the power to steal your peace or joy. Only your response to them and the way you choose to relate to God during them can do that.

Fear comes because of the way we perceive and process trouble. It's based on what's happening *in* you, not *to* you. As people of faith, we can possess our souls. We can choose to be led by the Spirit and walk through every circumstance by faith. First John 4:18 says, *"There is no fear in love; but perfect love casts out fear, because fear involves torment. But he who*

As a believer, the problems you're dealing with do not have the power to steal your peace or joy. Only your response to them and the way you choose to relate to God during them can do that.

fears has not been made perfect in love." God's love casts worry, anxiety, and fear from our hearts. It speaks to us amid trouble and reminds us of His love (see 1 John 4:8). And when we come to Him, taking His yoke of love upon ourselves, we learn even more of that love and suddenly realize that fear is gone.

According to Dictionary.com, *fear* is "a distressing emotion aroused by impending danger, evil, or pain whether the threat is real or imaginary." Much of the fear happening in our hearts and going on in our world is not based in reality. It's built on assumptions, imaginary scenarios, and lies. It comes by letting our imaginations run wild and worrying about the future. We wonder why our lives are going in the wrong direction, never realizing we've given place to strongholds and are now imprisoned by fear (see Prov. 4:23; 18:20-21). God wants us to harness those thoughts and imaginations, to *"bringing into captivity every thought ... to the obedience of Christ"* so we can experience His peace (2 Cor. 10:5).

It doesn't matter what you're going through. With the right perspective and relationship to God's grace, you can overcome. The devil won't be able to stress you out when you face challenges. Instead, you will experience God's faithfulness and learn to stretch your faith. One of the ways I learned to relate to God (and my problems) properly was to consider the eternal outcome and how I can stay yoked up to Jesus between then and now.

As a Christian, I ask myself, "What is the worst that could happen?" Death. Death is the fear that Satan used to hold humanity in bondage for thousands of years (see Heb. 2:15). But Jesus delivered us from the fear of death at His resurrection. He took the sting out of death by bearing our sins on the cross and robbed the grave of victory by His resurrection (see 1 Cor. 15:55). For a believer, death is easy. It's a shadow, a crossing over into God's manifest presence, guiltless and free of wrath. Psalm 23:4 (KJV) says, *"Yea though I walk through the valley of the* ***shadow*** *of death, I will fear no evil, for You are with me."* David spoke of death in terms of a shadow. A shadow does not have substance.

First Corinthians 15:56 says, *"The sting of death is sin, and the strength of sin is the law."* Sin has no more strength because of Jesus fulfilling the law on our behalf and bearing our sin in His body on the tree (cross). He took the substance of our sin, taking the sting out of death, making it but a shadow we pass through. When I died during bypass surgery and went to heaven, there was no sting or pain in dying. I went straight into the presence of Jesus and experienced nothing but love and peace. There was absolutely no fear or guilt, just love and acceptance. If the Lord tarries, we will all die. But when Jesus returns to this earth, He will bring us back with Him. Our bodies will be raised immortal, incorruptible, and we will never face death again. Death is not something to fear. It is something to prepare for and face with faith in God's promises.

That's what Paul was referring to when he said,

> *For our light affliction, which is but for a moment, is working for us a far more exceeding and eternal weight of glory, while we do not look at the things which are seen, but at the things which are not seen. For the things which are seen are temporary, but the things which are not seen are eternal.*
>
> 2 Corinthians 4:17-18

When I died during bypass surgery and went to heaven, there was no sting or pain in dying. I went straight into the presence of Jesus and experienced nothing but love and peace.

Our problems are temporal, God's promises are eternal.

What perspective are we going to take on the issues of this life? Are we going to focus on only those things we can see? *"To be absent from"* our bodies (death) is *"to be present with the Lord"* (2 Cor. 5:8). And while we fight physical death as an enemy of what we can accomplish for God's Kingdom, when our race is done, death becomes our gain (see Phil. 1:21). The world doesn't understand this hope.

Over the last few years, it appears COVID-19 and the possibility of death has been used to empower some and enslave the masses. It was said, if we didn't wear masks, social distance, quarantine, and get vaccinated over and over again, we would die (or at least cause others to die). There seemed to be no concern for the loss of freedom or careers. No care for personal sovereignty or mental health. No concern over children's education or the economic hardship of millions. And it was all perpetrated in the name of compassionate science. But there was no science on mask or vaccine efficacy. There couldn't be because there was no data or even enough time to gather data. Pure science will be studying the effects of masks and vaccines for years. I'm certain that if the facts do not match the political narrative of the day, those facts will be suppressed and censored even as they are today. No one really knows what the possible consequences will be on the body and immune system. Even now, cases of heart issues, blood clots, and unexplained deaths among young people are surfacing. And still, the fearmongering continues. To even ask questions, which is a tenant of science, is to be mocked and censored. The lust for power and control has consumed the powers that be and to oppose them and their fear tactics can be costly.

It is heartbreaking to see how many people willfully relinquished their freedom during this time—even more so, the number of Christians who responded to this event in fear. We must learn from this dress rehearsal of deception and prepare for what's next. We must choose to respond to the events of our world with God's Word in faith, defend truth, and resist the lies that foster fear. If you found yourself living in fear for the last few years, I am not condemning you. I want to encourage you. Fear is a spirit. But so is faith (see 2 Cor. 4:13). And as people of faith, we are called to live in faith.

God has not given us a spirit of fear, but of power and of love and of a sound mind.

2 Timothy 1:7

I will not be led by fear. Nor will I be manipulated by any powers that try to impose fear on others. Fear is not of God; fear-based decisions always lead to bondage and the loss of freedom. But God gave us the tools we need to fight it in faith—power, love, and a sound mind.

We must choose to respond to the events of our world with God's Word in faith, defend truth, and resist the lies that foster fear.

Years ago, a friend of mine who likes to give me a hard time, asked me to join him for a deer hunt on a private ranch in South Texas in November of 1988. Because I love to hunt and this would be a new place for me, I accepted the invitation and took my family for a mini-vacation. The first few days of the hunt, my friend and his family were teasing me in good fun. And I was dishing it back just as quickly as I could, never allowing them to have the last laugh. (I don't start these things, but I do hit back in good Christian fun.) On one occasion, we split up for a morning hunt. They went to one side of the ranch to hunt, and I went to the other. After a while, I heard guns going off. It sounded like World War III on the other side of the ranch, and soon enough one of the guys came speeding up in a Jeep. "Preacher!" he shouted. "You've got to come see this!"

Without thinking, I climbed into the Jeep, and we raced off to the other side of the ranch. I decided they must have come across a whole herd of hogs and needed my help. When we reached our destination, the guy hopped out, and I followed. He ran to a little ledge and jumped, turning slightly left as he landed. Again, I followed. But when I jumped off the ledge, I didn't turn left. I went straight down—and landed at the edge of a rattlesnake patch!

Now, I am not afraid of man or beast, but I have an awesome respect for snakes. Snakes bite. And nine diamondback rattlesnakes bite ... bite ... bite. And bite some more. I was (to put it mildly) freaking out! Emotions poured out of me. Emotions I didn't know I had. I was overloaded, overcharged. And you can bet your boots my mind was racing for answers. "Why was I in this horrible situation? Who put me in it? And how am I going to get out?" Now, before I go on with my story, let me be clear, I was in no real harm or danger, nor were my friends being as mean as this sounds.

Before I could completely process what was happening, I heard my friends up on that ledge having a good laugh at my expense. For me, there is no sound more paralyzing than that of a rattling rattlesnake, and at the time I did not appreciate their sense of humor. Nothing about being in the middle of a patch of poisonous snakes at that moment seemed funny. It took me a few seconds to realize the snakes had no heads. It was unseasonably warm that day, and apparently, one of the guys had come across a rattlesnake sunning itself on a rock. Startled, he took a shot. The snake zipped back into its den, and he called everyone over. These snakes were a real problem on this ranch and a real danger to the children and grandchildren that visited. So, they poured gasoline into the den so the snake would come out, and they could kill it. Only nine rattlesnakes came slithering out instead.

One of the snakes was over six feet long. Two or three were over five feet, and the rest were at least four feet long. My friend and his family were prepared. They shot off all the snakes' heads (which was what I'd heard on the other side of the ranch) and concocted this plot to tease the preacher. So, when I came charging in expecting a herd of hogs (and an awesome hunting story), I couldn't have fallen into their plan more perfectly. You see, even though the snakes were headless, their bodies were still moving. And while my eyes could see that the snakes were headless, the sound of their rattles had engaged my emotions and blocked my brain's ability to process what I saw. I needed to harness my thoughts to the reality that those snakes posed no threat to me. They couldn't harm me, but fear could. Fear might have driven me to fall off the ledge or damage my body trying to get away. It could have given me a heart attack. It took a moment, but with patience, I possessed my soul and got control of my emotions. Then, I was determined to fight back. Fear would not get the best of me. And those men would not have the last laugh. So, I reached down with one arm and grabbed a rattlesnake. Its writhing body wrapped itself around my arm. I reached down with the other and grabbed another snake. It, too, wrapped itself around my arm. And with my massive, Arnold Schwarzenegger-like arms, I turned to face those precious brothers with a yell of triumph and the best bodybuilder pose I could muster. Truth triumphed over fear, and I got the last laugh.

Chapter Six

GARDENING THE HEART

Don't worry about anything; instead,
pray about everything.

Philippians 4:6 (NLT)

In Genesis 3:15, God promised Adam and Eve that though they had failed to protect the Garden of Eden and follow in His way, a rescuer was coming through "her Seed." Women don't have seed; men do, so Messiah's birth had to be supernatural. And though the serpent would bruise the Messiah's heel, Messiah would crush his head.

Jesus was born of a virgin. The seed of His birth came from the Word of God and Mary's faith in that Word (Luke 1:38; 1 Pet. 1:23). And though the religious leaders of Jesus' time did not expect Messiah to rescue the world through His death, His death fulfilled this prophecy that the serpent, Satan, would bruise His heel (crucifixion). And Jesus' resurrection crushed the devil's head.

Hebrews 2:14-16 (KJV) declares:

Forasmuch then as the children are partakers of flesh and blood, he also himself likewise took part

> *of the same; that through death he might destroy him that had the power of death, that is, the devil; and deliver them who through* ***fear of death*** *were all their lifetime subject to bondage. For verily he took not on him the nature of angels; but he took on him the seed of Abraham.*

Jesus became a man to conquer death and release humanity from fear's tyranny. Satan has no more power or authority. He cannot hurt you. He is like one of those dead snakes I encountered while hunting. All he can do is rattle and inspire fear, hoping that you voluntarily yield to it. Don't. Don't allow fear to ensnare you. Recognize that God is with you no matter what rattling you hear. Pull out those Schwarzenegger-arms and remind yourself that *"greater is he that is in you, than he that is in the world"* (1 John 4:4 KJV). Let God's Word replace your fear with faith and your worry with hope. Take up whatever fear-serpent you encounter and trust that nothing shall by any means harm you (see Mark 16:18).

The word *destroy* in Hebrews 2 means "to be entirely idle; to make void" (G2673). By becoming human, living sinlessly, dying on the cross, and being raised from the dead, Jesus made null and void the fear of death that once enslaved humanity. He did not eradicate death, at least not yet. Nor did He annihilate Satan to where Satan can't even rattle—that day is coming. But Jesus rendered both death and Satan powerless in our lives. For the Christian, *"to live is Christ. and to die is gain"* (Phil. 1:21).

We live knowing that God is working everything together for our good and His eternal purpose (see Rom. 8:28). And if we die, we see Him face-to-face. No more darkness. No more evil. No more sorrow, sickness, or pain (see Rev. 21:4). For the believer, this life is a win-win scenario. We either die and go to be with Jesus, or God works everything together for our good in this life. That's it. That's our worst-case scenario. And that's how we are to process everything we go through in this life.

This reframing of hardship and affliction replaces worry with hope and helps us endure life's challenges. It allows us to stretch our faith instead of becoming stressed and overloaded in our hearts. Worry is the twin sister to fear. It is a negative imagination and only believes the worst. It's that feeling that nothing is going to work out for our good and is ultimately a form of unbelief.

Worry is the twin sister to fear.

We were not created for worry. Yet, many born-again, Spirit-filled believers worry all the time. My mother was a champion worrier, and it messed her up so much she thought love and worry were synonymous. If I didn't worry about her, that meant I didn't love her. If I didn't worry about my siblings, I didn't love them. That's wrong. `

Worry is the absence of hope (see Prov. 13:12; 29:18). But we serve a *"God of hope"* who offers hope—the image of a good outcome—in every situation we face (Rom. 15:13). Setting our hope on God and His promises eliminates worry. (You can't worry and hope at the same time.) So, if fear and worry try to minister to you, resist them. Guard your heart (like Adam was supposed to guard the Garden of Eden) and refuse to let them steal your hope.

In the first creation, Adam was assigned to guard and to garden Eden. To *"dress it and to keep it"* (Gen. 2:15 KJV). His failure unleashed fear and brought sin and death to the whole world. Jesus, the second man and last Adam, was sent to make all things new—to right the wrongs of that first man and bring us back to God's original design (1 Cor. 15:45-47).

After Jesus' resurrection, when the new creation had been completed, notice how He was revealed. Mary Magdalene had visited Jesus' tomb and discovered that its stone had been rolled away. Jesus' body was missing. Assuming someone had broken in and stolen His body, she wept. Suddenly, Jesus appeared behind her, but she did not recognize Him. Jesus asked why she was crying and who she was seeking, and John recorded Mary's answer as, *"Supposing Him to be the gardener,* [she] *said to Him, 'Sir, if you have carried Him away, tell me where you have laid Him, and I will take Him away'"* (John 20:15). Mary saw Jesus as a gardener. It wasn't until He called her by name that she realized who He was. This seemingly insignificant moment shows us that Jesus, as the second Adam, had become Gardener of the new creation (see1 Cor. 3:9; 2 Cor. 5:17).

When we come to Jesus (the Gardener of our hearts), yoke up to Him, and learn of Him, we mix faith with His grace. We partner in the overseeing of our hearts as we nurture what is good (the seeds of God's Word) and deal with what is not (the weeds of lies, anxiety, worry, and fear). When we ignore these rhythms of grace, we stop guarding our hearts, and they become occupied with meaningless, temporal issues (see Heb. 13:9). We cease partnering with Jesus and soon find things growing in our hearts that must be weeded out (see Prov. 4:23).

> *Therefore I say to you, do not worry about your life, what you will eat or what you will drink; nor about your body, what you will put on. Is not life more than food and the body more than clothing? Look at the birds of the air, for they neither sow nor reap nor gather into barns; yet your heavenly Father feeds them. Are you not of more value than they?*
>
> **Matthew 6:25-26**

Sad to say, many do not believe that we are of more value than animals. We have devalued human life for decades. Your value to God was worth the very life of Jesus. Never doubt His love and care for you.

"But," Jesus goes on to say, *"Seek first the kingdom of God and His righteousness, and all these things shall be added to you"* (Matt. 6:33). This entire discourse in Matthew 6 is the antidote for worry. When we seek God's Kingdom first and make His way our only option, we limit our thoughts to those of hope.

Your value to God was worth the very life of Jesus. Never doubt His love and care for you.

My life got drastically easier when I began "seeking first" God's Kingdom. When I let His Word make my choices and direct my thoughts, it knocked anxiety, worry, and stress out the door. I could no longer choose to be weak. God's Word had commanded me to *"be strong in the Lord and in the power of His might"* (Eph. 6:10). As a man crucified with Christ, I couldn't choose to be faithless or afraid. God's Word commanded me to have faith and courage (see Josh. 1:6). Suddenly, my imagination filled with hope, and I realized I'd been carrying around a messiah complex.

Many preachers collapse under the weight of ministry because they try to be all things to all people (and not in the way Paul meant). They take on God's responsibility to change hearts, fix circumstances, and right behaviors when doing so is impossible. We can't change other people. As a preacher, my responsibility is to speak the truth in love. What you choose to do with it is between you and God.

If you're trying to change your spouse, your kids, or others, you're carrying a weight that's too heavy for you. Remove some of life's stress and let go of your messiah complex. You can't change your spouse. You can't even change yourself without God's help. Allow God to change them. Stop trying to control your kids. Don't carry around a sense of guilt over the decisions your adult children are making outside your home. Pray for them. Love them. And give them to God. Only He can change their hearts.

If you're in the ministry, remember that you are an under-shepherd in God's house. You are not *the* Shepherd. You are not people's savior. If it takes *"fear and trembling"* to *"work out your own salvation,"* what makes you think you can work out someone else's (Phil. 2:12)? You cannot convict, convince, or convert anyone to the truth. Only the Holy Spirit can do that. You just speak the truth in love and let God's Word do the work.

When we try to change others or ourselves (or even our circumstances) through our own effort or wisdom, we frustrate grace. Paul encountered this problem in the church at Galatia and mentioned it in His letter to them several times.

> *I am crucified with Christ: nevertheless I live; yet not I, but Christ liveth in me: and the life which I now live in the flesh I live by the faith of the Son of God, who loved me, and gave himself for me. I do not* ***frustrate the grace*** *of God: for if righteousness come by the law, then Christ is dead in vain.*
>
> Galatians 2:20-21 (KJV)

> *You have become estranged from Christ, you who attempt to be justified by law; you have* ***fallen from grace****.*
>
> Galatians 5:4

The phrase *"fallen from grace"* here is not a label for a preacher caught in sin. Grace is God's power to change us regardless of our weakness (see 2 Cor. 12:8). We "fall from grace" every time we look to something besides Jesus' finished work to be used, blessed, or accepted by God. When we look to the law for righteousness with God, we "fall from grace." Sin does not frustrate grace. Self-effort and pride frustrate grace. Looking to the law for righteousness and blessings from God frustrates God's grace while humility (submission to God) gives us *"more grace"* (James 4:6-7). Or as Paul said,

"Where sin abounded grace did much more abound" (Rom. 5:20). When we fall into sin of any measure or kind, God's grace abounds toward us. God is merciful and extends love and mercy toward us in our weaknesses.

> *Let us therefore come boldly to the throne of grace, that we may obtain mercy and* ***find grace*** *to help in time of need.*
>
> Hebrews 4:16

There is no greater time of need than when we fall or fail in righteousness. Grace cannot be earned or deserved. But it must be found. Noah *"found grace"* to build the ark (see Gen. 6:8). Lot *"found grace"* to be delivered from Sodom and Gomorrah (see Gen. 19:19). Joseph *"found grace"* as a slave in Egypt (see Gen. 39:4 and Acts 7:10). Moses *"found grace"* to lead the Israelites out of captivity (see Exod. 33:17). Gideon found grace when he questioned God's call (see Judg. 6:17-23). Mary found grace to bear the Son of God (see Luke 1:30). Stephen found grace as he was being stoned for his testimony about Jesus (see Acts 7:55). And Paul found grace on his way to persecute the Church (see Acts 9:15; 1 Tim. 1:14). Each of these people found the grace of God in their time of need. They found grace when they were weak, not

When we fall into sin of any measure or kind, God's grace abounds toward us. God is merciful and extends love and mercy toward us in our weaknesses.

when they were strong. Regardless of what you're going through or what you have done, grace is available to you. And you find that grace at the throne of Jesus. You find it in prayer as you come to Jesus.

Years ago, I considered quitting the ministry. People's pain, both of their own making and that of others, was affecting me. So were the numbers of people who got angry or offended at me for no apparent reason. I didn't understand that persecutions and afflictions come with the gospel message. I wasn't prepared for the pushback I got for sharing God's morals and holiness, for speaking truth in love in a world of lies. And I didn't think I had the emotional makeup to deal with the opposition and meanness of people. I wanted to be known as a kind person. I wanted to remain compassionate and merciful, not become angry and bitter as some other preachers I knew had become. I thought I'd have to harden my heart to stay in ministry, and I didn't want to do that. Then, the Lord spoke to me from Isaiah 41.

> *Fear not [there is nothing to fear], for I am with you; do not look around you in terror and be dismayed, for I am your God. I will strengthen and* ***harden you to difficulties****, yes, I will help you; yes, I will hold you up and retain you with My [victorious] right hand of rightness and justice.*
>
> Isaiah 41:10 (AMPC)

That verse was the grace of God to me in my time of need. It made it possible for me to keep going. God showed me

God showed me that if I would learn to relate to His rhythms of grace, He would harden me to difficulties, not people.

that if I would learn to relate to His rhythms of grace, He would harden me to difficulties, not people. And He has been faithful to that word. God can harden your heart to difficulties too. He can protect you from the stress and fear that often accompany hardship, and while He does not cause or will anything bad in your life, He can use those difficulties to stretch you and help you grow—if you relate to them properly. His grace is available to you in your time of need, and He will work *"all things"* together for your good (Rom. 8:28-29). Don't let the devil shift your focus off God and all He has called you to. Don't let him inspire worry and fear. Remember what Christ accomplished for you and be of good courage. This is our responsibility in the guarding and gardening of our hearts.

As Joshua was about to take over leading the children of Israel, God told him,

> *Moses My servant is dead. Now therefore, arise, go over this Jordan, you and all this people, to the land which I am giving to them.... Have I not commanded you? Be strong and of good courage; do not be afraid, nor be dismayed, for the Lord your God is with you wherever you go.*
>
> **Joshua 1:2, 9**

Can you imagine how Joshua must have been feeling at that moment? Moses was dead. Over two million people (who hadn't proven to be very good followers) awaited instruction. And God put you in charge with the words, *"Go* [into the land of giants]. *And don't be afraid.* [Though you can't see Me and have thus far only received instruction from Me via Moses—the dead guy] *I am with you."* Wow! If that was not a time of need in Joshua's life, I'm not sure what was. And yet, God was with him. Grace did strengthen him, and he did lead the Israelites into the Promised Land. He actually accomplished what Moses had failed to accomplish.

Like Joshua, we do not walk alone through any trial or tribulation, any circumstance we face. But it is up to us to *"be strong and of a good courage."* It is up to us to control our thoughts and cast fear aside, to see ourselves the way God sees us and walk in faith.

> *(For the weapons of our warfare are not carnal, but mighty through God to the pulling down of strongholds;) casting down imaginations and every high thing that exalteth itself against the knowledge of God, and bringing into captivity every thought to the obedience of Christ.*
>
> **2 Corinthians 10:4-5 (KJV)**

Worry is a thought trying to exalt itself against the knowledge of God. When the leaders of Israel went to spy out the land of Canaan under Moses, ten of the twelve spies came back with an evil report. Though the land indeed flowed *"with milk and honey,"* all they saw were its challenges and obstacles (Num. 13:27-29). Worry possessed their hearts and they said, *"We are not able"* (Num. 13:31). Without God, this was true, but they were not without God. Only Joshua and Caleb saw God's promise as final authority and brought back a good report declaring, *"We are well able to overcome it"* (Num. 13:30).

The ten disheartened spies saw themselves as *"grasshoppers"* against giants, and that negative imagination cost the Israelites forty years in the wilderness (Num. 13:32-33). Thoughts are important and our imagination matters. They're seeds that take root in our hearts and will eventually bring forth a harvest. Negative thoughts, like worry, grow into a harvest of doubt and fear. Positive thoughts, like hope in God's promises, grow into a harvest of faith and peace. Isaiah 26:3 says, *"You will keep him in perfect peace, whose mind is stayed on You, because he trusts in You."* Quit seeing yourself as a failure and see yourself as a victor in Christ. Cast down imaginations that don't line up with God's Word and set your hope on His faithfulness (see 2 Cor. 10:5).

Thoughts are important and our imagination matters. They're seeds that take root in our hearts and will eventually bring forth a harvest.

Hebrews 6:18 says, we *"lay hold of the hope set before us."* Hope is always before us. Like a seed, it's always future tense. And those seeds act like an anchor to our souls (see Heb. 6:19). They give our minds something good to hold on to and imagine. (Faith, on the other hand, is "now." It is the harvest on those seeds of hope.)

Worry causes our lives to drift on stormy seas of gloom and doom. Hope keeps us immovable and unshakable in the promises of God. Thoughts affect our imaginations. Our imaginations, in turn, affect our emotions, and our emotions affect our actions (see Prov. 23:7). So, since the fruit of our lives starts with a thought, let's make it a good one. Let's learn to take every thought captive. Instead of worrying about the future, let's return to the throne of grace in prayer. We will *"find grace"* there *"to help"* us in our *"time of need,"* and as we plant seeds of hope in God's Word, we will experience the peace and joy of a worry-free heart (Heb. 4:16). We will see ourselves as "giants" in Christ, well able to possess all of God's promises in Christ.

Chapter Seven

SOBRIETY OF HEART

Be sober, be vigilant; because your adversary the devil walks about like a roaring lion, seeking whom he may devour.

1 Peter 5:8

As I mentioned previously, overcoming worry and the stress of life requires that we guard and garden our hearts. In Luke 21, Jesus warned His disciples that the "signs of the time" would come. He described wars and rumors of wars, nation rising against nation, earthquakes, famine, pestilence, and persecution—all things that are happening around us right now. And just like the disciples, we must guard our hearts to keep these things in their proper perspective and maintain a fear-free heart. In verse 31, Jesus said, *"When you see these things happening, know that the kingdom of God is near."*

Great opposition comes when God's Kingdom is near. But do you realize the Kingdom of God is in your heart? It's within all who are willing to yield to Jesus. So, we should not be perplexed when we experience opposition from other kings and kingdoms of this world.

Great opposition comes when God's Kingdom is near. But do you realize the Kingdom of God is in your heart?

Jesus continued by saying: *"Verily I say unto you, This generation shall not pass away, till all be fulfilled"* (Luke 21:32 KJV). That is profound. Jesus clearly told His disciples that everything He spoke of would be fulfilled before that generation passed away. Now, I'm not saying there aren't prophetic overtones concerning the things Jesus mentioned here that may still come to pass. I am saying that Jesus was specifically speaking to and preparing His disciples in this passage, just as He is speaking to and preparing us today.

Immediately following this warning, Jesus said, *"Heaven and earth shall pass away, but my words shall not pass away. And take heed to yourselves..."* (Luke 21:33-34 KJV). *"Take heed"* to yourself; in other words, mind your own business and pay attention to the guarding of your own heart. People are stressed out and filled with anxiety, worry, and fear because they take heed to everyone and everything but themselves. Dump that. Release your anxiety to God and follow Paul's advice, *"Study to be quiet, and to do your own business, and to work with your own hands, as we commanded you"* (1 Thess. 4:11 KJV).

Finishing, Jesus said:

> *And take heed to yourselves, lest at any time your hearts be overcharged with surfeiting, and drunkenness, and cares of this life, and so that day come*

> *upon you unawares. For as a snare shall it come on all them that dwell on the face of the whole earth.*
>
> **Luke 21:34-35 (KJV)**

Jesus said three things that overcharge the heart: surfeiting (gorging or overindulging in something), drunkenness, and the cares of this life. Our hearts were not created for such things—physically or spiritually. But in this context, when we talk about the heart, we're talking about the inner man, not the physical organ. According to Scripture, the inner man includes both your soul (your mind, will, and emotions) and your spirit (your new man in Christ). In some Scriptures, such as Ezekiel 36:26, the heart refers to your spirit man. *"I will give you a new heart and put a new spirit within you."* In others, *heart* refers to the soul. *"Out of the heart proceed evil thoughts, murders, adulteries, fornications, thefts, false witness.... These are the things which defile a man"* (Matt. 15:19-20). God's Word, in context, divides and discerns which is which (Heb. 4:12). According to *Strong's Concordance, kardia* (the word translated as both *heart* and *soul* in the New Testament) is "the thoughts or feelings; the middle" (G2588). The soul stands in the middle of spirit and body. It is like a bridge or mediator between the two. That's why Scripture says you cannot be *"carnally minded"* and *"spiritually minded"* at the same time (Rom. 8:6). The two don't mix.

Jesus said, if we fail to deal with the things that overcharge our hearts, *"that day will come upon us unawares."* What day is Jesus' talking about? The day of trouble. All of us face trouble in this life. We all face things we didn't plan for or see coming.

And if our hearts are not prepared for that day, the anxiety of that day will ensnare us and may even overtake our faith.

My mother was a good person, but after my brother died in a car accident and that pressure brought about an unwanted divorce, she fell apart. She could not cope with all the stress. She didn't know how to protect her heart and deal with the pain, and she became embittered. My heart also broke the day my brother died, and for four years, I experienced the *"day of trouble."* But in May of 1980, I had a supernatural encounter with Jesus that changed everything. He healed my, broken, overcharged heart, and set me on a journey of wholeness and fruitfulness of life. Jesus wanted the same for my mother. After all, He came to *"heal the brokenhearted"* (Isa. 61:1-2; Luke 4:18-19). But she didn't know how to relate properly to problems. For many years, she thought God was responsible for my brother's death, and if she allowed herself to forgive and heal, she would be dishonoring my brother's memory. Thankfully, after years of ministering to her, she relinquished that pain and came to Jesus on her deathbed.

We all face things we didn't plan for or see coming. And if our hearts are not prepared for that day, the anxiety of that day will ensnare us and may even overtake our faith.

I've been in ministry a long time and have met countless people who have fallen into the same trap my mother did—Christian and non-Christian alike. (In fact, I have never met anyone whose life is going so well they no longer needed the encouragement of church; they no longer needed to read the Word or pray.) Dear ones, when we don't prepare our hearts for the day of trouble and an unexpected death, divorce, or job loss comes, we are often overtaken. The same thing happens when a child suddenly goes off the rails or we face a betrayal. I get it. Those things are hard. They are discouraging. But as believers, we cannot allow them to shake our faith in a faithful God. When our hearts are bruised and we feel broken, we need encouraging relationships. We need connections where we can find help. And we need to prepare for those times by dealing with the three things Jesus said overcharge our hearts and lives—surfeiting, drunkenness, and the cares of this life.

SURFEITING

The word *surfeiting* appears only once in the King James Version of the Bible, and it's not really a word that comes up in casual conversation. According to the *Oxford Dictionary of English,* it means, "to consume too much of something." Surfeiting is "to indulge to excess in anything" (Dictionary.com). Merriam Webster defines it as, "to indulge to satiety in a gratification (such as indulgence of the appetite or senses). Surfeiting is literally self-indulgence. It is an indulgence in our senses. It is being controlled by our five physical senses. Surfeiting is when you make how you "feel" final and absolute authority. It doesn't matter what God says but rather "I feel this way!" Your appetites and senses become your god. We were not created to be self-centered, to sit around and think only about ourselves all day long. And while we do need to *"take heed to ourselves,"* there is a difference between that and being self-centered. Taking heed to yourself refers to judging yourself instead of others and focusing on your own spiritual growth and well-being. Self-centeredness is an attitude of "it's all about me and my needs and feelings." Such thinking is consumed with what's best for self, what will put self on top, or get self noticed. It thinks things like, *What will get me more "likes" on Facebook or clicks on YouTube.* Nothing else matters. This unhealthy focus on and love for self destroys families; it destroys churches and is a sign of the end times that leads to idolatry. *"But know this, that in the last days perilous times will come: For men will be* ***lovers of themselves*** *lovers of money ... lovers of pleasures more than lovers of God"* (2 Tim. 3:1-2).

Ultimately, self-centeredness is a sin of pride, the same sin that destroyed Sodom and Gomorrah, and got the devil kicked out of heaven (see Isa. 14:12-17; Ezek. 16:49). Its cure is humility. Humility is focusing on and submitting ourselves to Jesus and the Word. Humility recognizes that we aren't smart enough to run our lives. That without supernatural help, the natural appetites of our flesh become excessive and damage our lives and the lives of those around us. Galatians 5:22-23 speaks of the fruit of the Spirit, and one of them is temperance (self-control). One of the many byproducts (fruit) of God's Spirit in our lives is the discipline of self-control. True

Humility recognizes that we aren't smart enough to run our lives.

happiness comes from thinking of and serving others, not an unhealthy focus on self.

For example, we need food for strength, energy, and growth, but gluttony damages the body. *Gluttony* is an interesting word. When you look it up in Scripture, it has the overtones of a hangover. Proverbs 23:20-21 (NLT) says, *"Do not carouse with drunkards or feast with gluttons, for they are on their way to poverty, and too much sleep clothes them in rags."* Gluttony and drunkenness are running buddies that lead to no good. I have only overeaten a few times in my life, and I will never forget how nauseous and uncomfortable I felt. Other appetites of the flesh work the same way. Sex, for example, is a good thing. It's a gift from God. We were created sexual beings. But within that good gift of sexual love, God gave us boundaries. Sex, in the covenant of marriage, is healthy, wholesome, and lots of fun. It's awesome! But outside that boundary, sex can be one of the most destructive things in your life and culture. It quickly turns to lust, adultery, incest, pedophilia, rape, and other perversions that wreak havoc on your family legacy and society.

While sex and food are obvious examples, surfeiting can happen in any area of your life. Again, I'm not trying to condemn anyone who has found themselves in these places. We all have to search our hearts to keep from falling into these traps. Something happened to me a few years ago that prompted me to search my heart in this area. I lost my phone. My smartphone has become a valuable tool in life and ministry. I use it a lot, especially when I'm on the road. It is amazing what this little thing can do. With the touch of a button, I can connect with my elders, contact pastors and ministry relationships, study Scripture in several different translations, look up words in the dictionary or concordance, write sermon notes. It is an amazing resource. I also use my Bible app on my phone when I minister. It's the handiest thing. I have so many helpful apps on it and hundreds more available at my fingertips. It's awesome. But when I realized it was missing, a sense of panic came over me. That feeling was so strong I started to wonder if I was addicted to my smartphone. As I prayed and processed through this predicament, I realized it was the convenience I missed, not the phone itself. I used to carry a suitcase full of Bible translations and study materials when I traveled. It wouldn't be easy, but I knew I could go back to that method if I had to. Thankfully, I didn't have to. I found my phone—praise the Lord! —and am even more grateful for the convenience of technology. (That's my story, and I'm sticking to it!)

Jesus summed up this process in very simple terms. *"If anyone desires to come after Me, let him* ***deny himself****, and take up his cross and follow me"* (Matt. 16:24). Surfeiting is the opposite of denying self, and it leads to a drunkenness of heart. Self-centered people, people who think only of their needs and desires or who put their needs and desires over everything else, literally become intoxicated with their problems. Like alcoholics, they constantly return to the pains and disappointments of the past, drinking of their misery from sunup to sundown just like my Uncle Joe. They are drunk with offense. Drunk with pain. People who are drunk of heart can spend hours detailing their problems, but they can't concentrate on a godly solution for two minutes.

If we choose to meditate on hurts, problems, disappointments, and setbacks, it's like pouring alcohol into our bodies all day long. It's poisonous.

Dear ones, the things we choose to meditate on have lasting consequences in our lives (see Prov. 4:23). If we choose to meditate on hurts, problems, disappointments, and setbacks, it's like pouring alcohol into our bodies all day long. It's poisonous. We need to wake up from this drunken stupor and learn to live a life of sobriety—heart and soul.

DRUNK OF HEART

First Peter 5:8 says, *"Be sober, be vigilant; because your adversary the devil walks about like a roaring lion, seeking whom he may devour."* This verse isn't referring to sobriety of body (though I do recommend that). It's referring to a sobriety of the mind or inner man.

As I mentioned previously, I grew up with an alcoholic uncle. He was a good man, but his life was out of control. I didn't know it until much later, but my paternal grandfather was a professional moonshiner. He hid his stills in the mountains of Tennessee and made a living running moonshine. Allegedly, my grandfather was caught and killed by the feds in a raid, but all I knew growing up was that he died when my dad was around five. No one really talked about my grandfather, but some of his kids had problems with alcohol. I imagine they were introduced to it at an early age and grew up with it being a normal part of their lives. That's why my heart goes out to anyone dealing with addiction. I saw what it did to my Uncle Joe. I saw what it did to my mom. And I know what it could have done to me. I am very familiar with the symptoms of drunkenness and have nothing but mercy for those battling this issue. But dear ones, those same symptoms can happen to any of us—whether or not we ever become physically drunk. We can all become drunk in our hearts.

The top three symptoms of drunkenness that we need to be aware of and diligent against are confusion, poor judgment, and vulnerability. Let's look at these for a moment.

CONFUSED

A drunken heart is disoriented and confused. If you've ever been around someone who is drunk, they have no idea where they're going or what they're doing. That's what happens to us when our hearts get drunk on the affairs of life or the evil and pain of this world. There've been a few times in ministry that my own heart felt that way. Years ago, a member of the church came against me. This was very early in the ministry, and I was young. My leadership skills were still developing and maturing. I was so blindsided, and it hurt so deeply that I felt there was no reconciling over what was done, and I lost sound judgment. I allowed myself to become drunk of heart and resolved to simply resign in order to protect my family and keep peace within the church.

Sue was my first "sobriety station." We discussed what was happening, and though she disagreed with my solution, she was willing to support me if I chose to walk away. I checked in with several elders of the church, each independent of the other, who said the same thing. They didn't think resigning was God's best but were willing to support my decision to leave if they could go with me. Their love and commitment shook me out of my drunken stupor of the mind, and we were able to find a godly solution together. In this particular case, I stood up to the accuser and countered their accusations with the truth. They repented, I stayed, and God turned everything around for good.

I recommend everyone have these stations—these relationships and connections—where you can go to get off the crazy train of a drunken heart and regain a sense of sobriety and clear thinking. Were it not for these trustworthy people who loved and supported me, but could also give me a different perspective and help me process the hurt and confusion I was dealing with, things would not have turned out so well. The manifold grace of God within them helped me sober up and make a good decision when I was struggling to hear God amid the fear and pain.

POOR JUDGMENT

Have you ever watched a friend do a piece of stupid? If you're like me, your first thought is always, "What were they thinking?" And that's the problem. They weren't thinking. Like someone who's physically drunk, we can't think straight when we're drunk of heart. When someone gets drunk, good judgment and discretion go right out the window. Discernment becomes impaired, and they do things they wouldn't normally do.

Have you ever known someone shy and reserved until they've had a few drinks? Once they're drunk, they start doing all sorts of things they would never do while sober. They might dance on the table or pick a fight with someone they've never met. That's what happens when we get drunk of heart. We lose sound judgment and start making poor decisions. We do things that damage ourselves and others.

Liquid courage is not the same as Holy Ghost courage—and I'm not just talking about alcohol. When we become drunk of heart, we lose all sense of discernment and do and say things we later regret. We stop walking in wisdom and charge into situations with a "hold my beer" attitude. But the Word says, *"And be not drunk with wine* [or we could substitute "be not drunk of heart" here], *wherein is excess; but be filled with the Spirit"* (Eph. 5:18 KJV). Excess almost always leads to poor judgment and regret. It creates vulnerability in our lives and robs us of our effectiveness.

Liquid courage is not the same as Holy Ghost courage.

VULNERABLE

A drunken heart is a vulnerable heart. It is easily robbed of peace and joy. If a thief came across a strong man, he'd think twice before trying to steal his wallet. But if that thief were to get the man drunk, he could take the man's wallet without a fight. He could push the man over and even kick him while he's down. The man wouldn't be able to stop him. That's what

Satan is trying to do to you. He's trying to get you drunk of heart so that he can easily overtake you in the day of trouble.

Satan doesn't have any real power over you. Remember, Jesus crushed the head of the serpent through His death and resurrection. The devil cannot hurt you. He cannot steal from you, kill you, or destroy your effectiveness—unless he gets you drunk of heart. Then the cares of this life become overwhelming, worry and fear overcharge your heart and make the Word of God *"unfruitful"* (see Mark 4:19).

CARES OF THIS LIFE

If you're worried over whether or not you'll have a job tomorrow, if you're afraid your spouse will leave, or that your kids won't survive their immaturity, and you let that worry get into your heart, it will choke out the Word of God. You'll find yourself in a drunken stupor over things you cannot control and feel stuck in a cycle of confusion, poor judgment, and vulnerability. You need an intervention. You need someone to tell you to sober up. And that someone is me! Be of sober mind and heart so that when the day of trouble comes you can stand your ground. Continue to learn the rhythms of God's grace that keep your heart sober, and your life will become fruitful and productive.

Satan doesn't have any real power over you.

Chapter Eight

THE POWER OF HUMILITY

Take my yoke upon you. Let me teach you, because I am ***humble*** and gentle at heart, and you will find rest for your souls.

Matthew 11:29 (NLT)

When we come to Jesus and learn of Him, we discover true humility. True humility is a foreign concept to most people. While nearly everyone understands that humility is the opposite of pride, they seem to think of humility as putting themselves down. Yet Moses wrote in Numbers 12:3 that he was the meekest man on the face of the earth. *Meek* in this passage means humble. How could he say that and still be humble? Perhaps we don't truly understand humility. Scripture says that God is humble (see Matt. 11:29). He is not prideful. He doesn't do things for His own benefit but moves and acts on our behalf.

Pride, on the other hand, is self-centered. It is confidence in who we are independent of Christ. It can manifest as arrogance—thinking more highly of ourselves than we ought (see Rom. 12:3). "I'm smarter, faster, or better than you." Or it can manifest as self-depreciation: "Poor me. Woe is me. I'm nothing. I'm so unworthy. I ... I ... I." That's the way I lived early in my Christian walk. I wasn't arrogant, but I was self-centered. I thought putting myself down was humility. But all those negative thoughts and attitudes were really just pride. They were self-centered and developed within me a false sense of humility. It produced inferiority complexes and esteem issues.

True humility is God focused and others minded. It prefers others and lifts them up instead of putting them down. Though it acknowledges weakness, humility also accepts what God says as truth. It is confidence in *"Christ in you, the hope of glory"* (Col. 1:27). When God's Word says, *"I can do all things through Christ,"* humility accepts that (Phil. 4:13). When Jesus said, *"Without Me you can do nothing,"* humility accepts that too (John 15:5). True humility submits to God's Word. It lets God be true and every man—even yourself—a liar (see Rom. 3:4). A humble person accepts what God says regardless of circumstances, feelings, or opinions. A humble person is teachable and quick to repent. A humble person accepts God's Word as final authority.

Once I saw grace and true humility, I went from a low self-esteem (pride) to a high Christ-esteem (humility). I went from a negative self-image to a positive Christ-image (see Rom. 8:29). I went from inferiority complexes after my flesh to superiority complexes in Christ over sin, Satan, and the world (see 1 John 5:5). God's grace became sufficient and filled all my human weaknesses. I discovered that denying myself meant I had to take up the work of the cross in Christ (humility) and experience the power of God's grace to change my life (Matt. 16:24).

> *Likewise you younger people, **submit** yourselves to your elders. Yes, all of you be **submissive** to one another, and be clothed with **humility**, for "God resists the proud, but gives grace to the humble." Therefore humble yourselves under the mighty hand of God, that He may exalt you in due time, casting all your care upon Him, for He cares for you.*
>
> 1 Peter 5:5-7

Casting our care on God requires humility. It requires that we let go of our problems and relinquish control over their outcomes. Humility rests in the knowledge that God sees, God cares, and God will make things right. Pride encourages us to think we can work everything out on our own, that we don't need God or anyone else. Humility trusts that God will care for us better than we can care for ourselves. It recognizes our need for God and depends on Him and Him in others.

Casting our care on God requires humility. It requires that we let go of our problems and relinquish control over their outcomes.

Too often in our culture, dependency is looked upon as weakness. (And if our dependency is centered on man, that is probably true.) But dependency on God is not weakness. It's how we receive *"more grace"* (James 4:6). But humility is our responsibility. When humility recognizes error, it welcomes God's loving correction, knowing that His chastening will produce fruit and that, in time, He will exalt us. Submission is connected to humility. We learn to submit to God and His Word as well as others that God places in our lives. The younger can glean from the life experiences of an older generation or glean from spiritual elders and their Kingdom experiences.

Growing up in church, I remember being told to cast my care upon the Lord, and though I tried, every time I prayed, my care felt like a boomerang. I'd throw it up to the Lord, and it would come spinning right back down to me. I found myself meditating more on my problems than on God, and often I left my prayer time feeling worse than before I prayed. So, how do we cast our care on the Lord? How do we give the worry over our kids, the economy, or our retirement to the Lord in prayer? Peter showed us in the remainder of this passage.

He began in verse eight with, *"Be sober."* As I've said before, this isn't talking about not being drunk on alcohol—though that is also wise. Here, Peter was talking about being sober of heart. He also told us to be on guard—not just defensively, but offensively. *"Be sober, be vigilant."* We cannot be passive regarding Satan's schemes. Faith is not passive. James 4:7 says, *"Submit to God.* ***Resist*** *the devil and he will flee from you." Resist* means to "stand against or oppose," not to ignore, deny, or hole-up and wait (*anthistmi*, G436). But we cannot resist Satan until we first submit to God. Both of these actions are aggressive. They're how we fight the good fight of faith.

The rest of 1 Peter 5:8 says, *"Be sober, be vigilant; because your adversary the devil walks about like a roaring lion, seeking whom he may devour."* Notice that Peter did not say Satan "is" a roaring lion. The devil only walks about "like" a roaring lion. He has no real power. He's just a deceiver. Jesus pulled out the devil's teeth at the resurrection. Satan is just a pussycat trying to convince you and me that he's a big threat. He is *"seeking whom he may devour."* The devil can't devour you without your permission. We have to yield in temptation and sin or in deception. He has been stripped of his authority and now uses our God-given authority against us. Paul spoke of Satan getting an *"advantage"* over us, *"for we are not ignorant of his devices"* (2 Cor. 2:11). Paul also wrote in Ephesians 4:26-27, *"'Be angry, and do not sin': do not let the sun go down on your wrath, nor* ***give place*** *to the devil."* Notice that there is an anger that is not sin. We are to not let the sun go down on it. This anger is not of the flesh or sin but rather against Satan and evil. If you let the sun go down on evil, you will give Satan place in your life. Romans 12:9 says, *"Let love be without hypocrisy. Abhor what is evil. Cling to what is good."* A love that does not abhor evil and cleave to good is a hypocritical love, not the love of God. Peter continued:

Satan is just a pussycat trying to convince you and me that he's a big threat.

> ***Resist him****, steadfast in the faith, knowing that the same sufferings are experienced by your brotherhood in the world. But may the God of all grace, who called us to His eternal glory by Christ Jesus, after you have suffered a while, perfect, establish,*

> *strengthen, and settle you. To Him be the glory and the dominion forever and ever. Amen.*
>
> **1 Peter 5:9-11**

We resist the devil by submitting to the Word of God in humility. We do not yield to deception and trickery. We resist Satan's stratagems *"steadfast"* or immovable in our faith. We recognize that the pressure we're facing is not unique. Our brothers and sisters in the Lord are experiencing the same thing all over the world, and we learn to guard and garden our hearts during that affliction. When we do that, God's grace meets us in our weakness. It abounds toward us to strengthen, establish, and mature us in faith.

Other translations of these verses in 1 Peter use the phrase *"be sober minded"* or *"self-controlled."* These are references to clear thinking. Peter was basically saying, "Use the 'sound mind' God gave you!" (see 2 Tim. 1:7). Many have yielded their mind, will, and emotions to the devil to such an extent that they've fallen into a spiritual stupor. They may have done so innocently, but they've allowed their heart to be conformed to the standards of this world. And if they took a spiritual-breathalyzer test, they'd be sent straight to jail. They don't have sobriety of soul. And worse, many don't realize how toxic their mind and emotions have become. They need a detox.

Remember, Satan cannot overtake us unless we are drunk of heart. Just like people who physically detox are amazed at what comes out of their bodies and how much better they feel afterward, we must take the time to detox our souls. With all the darkness and evil in the world, it's easy for our hearts to become toxic and end up in a drunken stupor. And for most of us, it happens innocently. We get caught up in the day-to-day and forget to cast our care on the Lord. We allow that care to multiply and cause us to become overloaded, emotionally charged, and overwhelmed.

When we cast our care on the Lord, we unload our hearts. We fix our minds on Him and remember His goodness. Instead of complaining about our problems, we pray the answer to our problems—His promises—and thank Him for His faithfulness. This builds our faith and gives us the sober mind we need to displace worldly thoughts with God's thoughts (which we find in His Word). It drives out fear and replaces worry with hope and peace. Isaiah 26 says:

> *Thou wilt keep him in perfect peace whose* ***mind*** *is stayed on thee: because he* ***trusteth*** *in thee: Trust ye in the Lord for ever.*
>
> Isaiah 26:3-4 (KJV)

Notice the link between our thoughts and faith. A part of trusting God is the harnessing of our thoughts and setting them on God's promises and faithfulness.

If we aren't experiencing perfect peace, our minds are not really stayed on God.

If we aren't experiencing perfect peace, our minds are not really stayed on God. We may think they are. They may be on the Lord for a moment. But they're not *"stayed"* or fixed on God. They're fixed on our problems, on the cares of this life. They're carnal, and Romans 8:6 says that being *"carnally minded"* leads to death.

THE PATH OF DEATH

God used the prophet Isaiah to warn Israel about this path. God said to Isaiah:

> *Now go and write down these words. Write them in a book. They will stand until the end of time as a witness that these people are stubborn rebels who refuse to pay attention to the Lord's instructions. They tell the seers, "Stop seeing visions!" They tell the prophets, "Don't tell us what is right. Tell us nice things. Tell us lies. Forget all this gloom. Get off your narrow path. Stop telling us about your 'holy one of Israel.'"*
>
> **Isaiah 30:8-11 (NLT)**

Here Isaiah described what rebellion looks and sounds like. But these words don't just apply to Israel. They don't just apply to the time in which they were written. Isaiah's words are a witness to us too. The difference? Most of the believers I know do not reject God's Word in open rebellion. They simply don't know it (or don't know how to apply it). They are biblically illiterate and are perishing for a lack of knowledge, not the rejection of knowledge (see Hosea 4:6). They have not separated themselves from the world's way of thinking or renewed their minds in God's Word (Rom. 12:2; 2 Cor. 6:17). They have been conformed to this world instead of transformed by renewing their minds to God's Word.

Others, both in and out of the church, flat-out reject the truth. They say, "Stop telling us visions of the future if we don't repent. Don't tell us what is right. Tell us nice things." They want preachers to lie instead of hurting their feelings with the truth of God's Word or the error of our ways. If you're in a good church, this may be hard to believe, but it happens more often than it should. People don't want to be lovingly confronted with the truth. They don't want to feel uncomfortable. They tell their pastors, "Stop preaching about what's on the horizon! Stop telling us to repent. Stop saying that we're hurting our children and grandchildren with 'woke' culture. Stop telling us about the corruption in our government, the corruption in Hollywood, the corruption in our pulpits. Don't mention election fraud or the danger of electing people who hate God and the country they are called to serve. Stop talking about the consequences of massive government debt or telling us what you see coming if we don't repent. What do those things matter?" These people don't want to know God's stance on morality, justice, marriage, or family. They don't want to know how He defines good and evil. His path is too narrow. But Jesus said,

> *Enter by the narrow gate; for wide is the gate and broad is the way that leads to destruction, and there are many who go in by it. Because narrow is the gate and difficult is the way which leads to life, and there are few who find it.*
>
> Matthew 7:13-14

There is only one way to heaven—Jesus Christ and the cross. But there are many ways to hell. To speak that truth does not make me or any other preacher a religious bigot. It does not make us narrow-minded. It makes us a faithful witness. Only Jesus died for your sins. Only He offers you life. And only His Word is truth (see John 14:6). We need Jesus. We need preachers who are faithful witnesses to the truth and point us toward the narrow path—not just to secure our eternal salvation, but also as an example of how we are to live. For if we claim to be His people, we need to live as He called us to live—holy (see Lev. 19:2; 20:7; 1 Pet 1:15-16; 2 Cor. 6:16-18).

Isaiah went on to record God's response to this attitude of carnal mindedness.

> *This is the reply of the Holy One of Israel: "Because you despise what I tell you and trust instead in oppression and lies, calamity will come upon you suddenly—like a bulging wall that bursts and falls. In an instant it will collapse and come crashing down. You will be smashed like a piece of pottery—shattered so completely that there won't be a piece big enough to carry coals from a fireplace or a little water from the well." This is what the Sovereign Lord, the Holy One of Israel, says: "Only in* ***returning to me*** *and* ***resting in me***

Only Jesus died for your sins. Only He offers you life. And only His Word is truth.

> *will you be saved. In quietness and confidence is your strength."*
>
> **Isaiah 30:12-15 (NLT)**

Some people think this passage exemplifies God's wrath for breaking the law, but I believe it demonstrates what happens when we reject God's instructions and go our own way. Proverbs 14:12 (KJV) tells us, *"There is a way which seemeth right unto man, but the end thereof are the ways of death."* This death is not God's wrath, but the consequences of rejecting God's wisdom and instruction. It describes the harvest that will come if we keep sowing bad seeds and remain drunk of heart. The day of trouble comes—and suddenly. Galatians 6 warns us of seeds sown (good and bad) and the inevitable consequences on a harvest of those seeds. Galatians 6:8 says, *"For he who sows to his flesh* [own ways versus God's] *will* ***of his flesh reap corruption****, but he who sows to the Spirit will of the Spirit reap everlasting life."* Notice it is of our flesh we reap corruption, not God! God is not punishing us for our bad seeds sown. Any corruption we experience is of our flesh, not from God.

The only way to avoid this harvest is to return to God, not just to be born again. That's the first step. But daily, as we walk with and rest in Him, we must keep coming to Jesus. We must take His yoke upon us—submit ourselves to the truth—and learn of Him (see Matt. 11:28-30). We must walk the narrow path. Only there will we find *"quietness and confidence."* Only there will we know His peace.

This world is loud. It's full of voices (see 1 Cor. 14:10). To experience peace, we must learn to be still, to quiet our souls. Only

This world is loud. To experience peace, we must learn to be still, to quiet our souls.

then can we hear God's voice and find strength for the day of trouble (see Ps. 46:10).

Unfortunately, the Israelites did not return to God. They chose not to rest in Him. Isaiah 30:15-16 (NLT) says,

> *But you would have none of it. You said, "No, we will get our help from Egypt. They will give us swift horses for riding into battle." But the only swiftness you are going to see is the swiftness of your enemies chasing you!*

Throughout the Bible, Egypt is used as a type referring to the world. When we reject the Lord's instructions and the unforced rhythms of God's grace—when we refuse to come to Jesus, be yoked to Him, and learn of Him—our hearts become overcharged. Our enemies of fear and worry chase us down and overtake us. And if we do not repent, we become needless casualties in God's Kingdom. I don't want to see that happen to anyone, nor does God!

Let's humble ourselves. Let's receive God's Word as the truth and final authority. Let's cast our care on Him, fixing our eyes on Jesus, and surrender our problems to Him. Then we will experience sobriety of heart and become His disciples. We will walk His narrow path and live in quietness and strength, without fear.

Chapter Nine

AVOIDING SPOILAGE

Beware lest any man spoil you through philosophy and vain deceit, after the traditions of men, after the rudiments of this world, and not after Christ.

Colossians 2:8 (KJV)

In Colossians 2:8, Paul listed four things that spoil a believer's heart and life. These things are toxic to our faith and lead to a life of worry and fear instead of hope and faith. *"Beware lest any man spoil you,"* he said. The word *spoil* here means "to lead away as booty," as in a pirate plundering and pillaging a ship (G4812). The four poisons Paul shared lead our hearts away from Christ. They pull us from the rhythms of grace found in Matthew 11, and they gradually spoil our lives. When something spoils, like milk left on a counter for too long, it slowly goes from good to bad. Think about that. How many Christians start their faith journey with joy, only to be spoiled by the world and its philosophies? Satan spoils them with philosophy and vain deceit, plundering their lives of the wonderful treasures offered us in Christ.

Philosophy, vain deceit, the traditions of men, and the rudiments of this world are influences that drive our world—things like the love of money and love for self—steal our inheritance in Christ. It's not that God withholds any good thing from us, but we become spoiled. That's why it's so important to be *"rooted and built up in"* Christ, to be taught the truth that is in Christ and become firmly *"established in the faith"* (Col. 2:7). We want to avoid the natural progression of spoilage that comes from living in and being saturated by the world (Eph. 4:20-24). Let's look more closely at the four toxins Paul described.

PHILOSOPHIES

Philosophy is simply a way of thinking. In Colossians 2:8, *philosophy* refers to man's thoughts, opinions, and wisdom independent of God (which the Bible calls *foolishness*). People, today, think they are wiser and even more righteous than God. Their philosophies regarding the origins of man, when life begins, how governments should work, sexuality and gender, and what happens after death are contrary to the Word of God and toxic to the human heart. These philosophies pull us away from truth. They spoil us and create uncertainty, worry, and fear in life.

"Climate change," for example, has been heralded as the end of the world and used as a scare tactic to force drastic measures in conservation and energy reform for decades. (When I was a kid, it was warnings about "the next ice age." But when the world started getting warmer instead of colder, it was changed to "global warming." Now, with the last few years of record low temperatures, it has switched to "climate change." Different terminology, same tactic.) Its goal is power, the loss of individual freedom, and government-mandated control. It is the only way to transition from a representative republic to a communist dictatorship without a bullet fired. It all leads to fear and the loss of freedom—freedom of speech, thought, movement, and career choices, just to mention a few. Today, the young people raised under this philosophy have no hope for marriage, family, and long, productive lives. The evils of abortion, infanticide, and euthanasia make sense to them as a means of population control and conservationism.

Many other such philosophies are spoiling generations in and out of the Church. But there is good news! God also has a way of thinking, and His way is unchanging. It isn't motivated by fear, nor does it create uncertainty in our lives. God's philosophy, His way of thinking, is found in His Word. Genesis 8:22 tells us, *"'While the earth remains, seedtime and harvest, cold and heat, winter and summer, and day and night shall not cease.'"* The earth will remain and cycle through cold and heat, day and night for as long as God determines (see Heb. 1:3). You and I can neither destroy nor save God's creation. To think otherwise is the apex of pride and a messiah complex.

Unfortunately, many come to Jesus and never renounce pride. They do not change their personal philosophy and submit to God's Word. In Isaiah 55:7, we read, *"Let the wicked forsake his way, and the unrighteous man* ***his thoughts****; let him return to*

God also has a way of thinking, and His way is unchanging.

the Lord, and He will have mercy on him; and to our God, for He will abundantly pardon." When we come to Jesus, we must not only forsake our wicked ways, but also set aside our unrighteous thoughts. Unrighteous thoughts are not just evil or perverted thoughts, but one contrary to the truth of God's Word. We can't keep thinking like we did before getting saved and experience peace. We must renounce worldly thoughts and wash our brains with the water of God's Word (see Eph. 5:26).

First Corinthians 1:18-20 (NLT) reads,

> *The message of the cross is foolish to those who are headed for destruction! But we who are being saved know it is the very power of God. As the Scriptures say, "I will destroy the wisdom of the wise and discard the intelligence of the intelligent." So where does this leave the philosophers, the scholars, and the world's brilliant debaters? God has made the wisdom of this world look foolish.*

God's Word has something to say about every philosophy in our culture. His Word brings the foolishness of man's so-called wisdom to light. And while it may take time to uproot, tear down, and rebuild the philosophies we had before knowing Christ, that's what it means to make Jesus Lord.

Second Corinthians 10:5 calls these worldly philosophies *strongholds* or *arguments* and tells Christians to cast them down by *"bringing every thought to the obedience of Christ."* The strongholds of sin and evil can only happen in our culture when we refuse to bring every philosophy of man to the obedience of Christ. God wants to reverse this—starting with His Church—but we need to renew our minds (change our philosophy) to God's way of thinking.

VAIN DECEIT

Vain deceit is fraud or outright lies. Fraud poisons the minds of innocent people and is motivated by a lust for power. It's how Satan, the father of lies, infuses our society with fear and usurps control (see John 8:44). Recently, the devil used lies surrounding COVID-19 to create panic over our health. He's also used election fraud, religious fraud, media fraud, and science fraud to pull people away from Christ. He has spoiled the Christian's faith in God's Word and God's good plan for humanity.

Take, for example, our national news media. How could so many different news outlets in different cities with different anchors read from the same page of election fraud? How could the false accusation of Russian collusion in the 2016 presidential election remain in the hearts and minds of millions after it had been proven false? Only through demonic influence, and if your only source of information was (and is) the national news media, you're in danger of spoilage.

To ensnare the masses, one must lie, lie often, and lie with impunity as he suppresses the truth. There is absolutely no negative consequences for lying, but there are rewards for deceiving the masses. It is hard to conceive how many people want to be lied to. That's why censorship and political correctness are so evil. There is a coordinated assault on truth from every corner of society. But the Church is called to be *"the pillar and ground of the truth"* (1 Tim. 3:15). We must love and embrace truth in these last days. We must pursue it and share it with a lost and dying world. Romans 1:18 says, *"For the wrath of God is revealed from heaven against all ungodliness and unrighteousness of men, who* ***suppress*** *the truth in unrighteousness."* The New Living Translation uses the word *"wickedness."* Vain deceit locks people into death and immaturity. It spoils, while the truth preserves.

Jesus prayed, *"Sanctify them by Your truth. Your word is truth"* (John 17:17). God's Word is truth. Period. It wasn't truth "in its time." It isn't truth only meant for some. It's not subjective. It is truth! It's objective and eternal. It doesn't change with culture. The Word is the only way for us to be sanctified. *Sanctify* means to be set apart or made holy (G37). It means to be purified. Sanctification in God's Word is how we detox our hearts and consecrate our minds so we can combat the lies of this culture. Jesus also said, *"If you abide in My word, you are My disciples indeed. And you shall know the truth, and the truth shall make you free"* (John 8:31-32). Knowing the truth sets the captive free. And when received in humility, God's Word has a cleansing effect. It sanctifies us and sets us free from the principalities and powers of darkness. When we submit to its final and absolute authority, the Word changes our minds and keeps us from being spoiled. Unfortunately, most believers continue in the

God's Word is truth. Period. It wasn't truth "in its time." It isn't truth only meant for some. It's not subjective. It is truth!

news media instead of God's Word, and those lies enslave them to worry and fear. Vain deceit spoils them to the truth and locks them into immaturity. We must come to Jesus—the truth—and keep coming to Him, stay yoked to Him, and learn of Him to avoid spoilage (see Eph. 4:21).

TRADITIONS OF MEN

Tradition in and of itself is not bad. Wholesome family traditions can be healthy. They can build family bonds. Paul spoke of healthy traditions, *"Therefore brethren, stand fast and hold the traditions which you have been taught, whether by word or our epistle"* (2 Thess. 2:15). But when those traditions no longer serve their original, godly purpose and become a matter of going through the motions, they morph into the traditions of men and are no longer healthy. Jesus said these types of traditions make God's Word *"of no effect"* (Mark 7:13). Singing from church hymnals, like many traditions, started as a blessing. They started with the intention of pointing people to Christ, but when that tradition was exalted above God or truth—when no other songs were considered holy or worthy of being sung—it became an idol.

Ways of thinking or acting that cannot be touched or challenged fall into this category. For example, if you vote a particular way because that's the way your family always voted (even if that way no longer reflects your Judeo-Christian values), your voting has morphed into a tradition of man. It has become an idol and will make the Word of God *"of no effect"* in your life (see 1 Cor. 10:19-20).

When dealing with the Pharisees, Jesus quoted Isaiah who said, *"These people honor me with their lips, but their hearts are far from me. Their worship is a farce, for they teach man-made ideas as commands from God"* (Mark 7:6-7 NLT). The New King James Version goes on to say in verse nine, "All too well you reject the commandment of God, that you may keep your tradition." When tradition becomes unassailable, it grows toxic and starts spoiling our hearts. It pulls us away from Christ and cancels out the power of God's Word.

Years ago, in the beginning stages of Victory Life Church, I canceled Sunday night services and moved our midweek service to Thursday nights. The decision was made with much prayer and godly counsel, but you would have thought I killed the Pope! People had a fit. They couldn't understand how changing service times would serve the vision God had given us for Victory Life. By changing Sunday nights to life group nights (small groups that gather in homes to pray, discuss the Word, build community, and fellowship), we could expand ministry opportunities throughout the city while giving people the margin of time needed for that. This solution also allowed me to minister in different churches without neglecting my flock, and allowed the community to visit our church and receive teaching they might not otherwise receive. This "tradition" served our church well for several

When tradition becomes unassailable, it grows toxic and starts spoiling our hearts. It pulls us away from Christ and cancels out the power of God's Word.

years, but we have since moved back to Wednesday night services as a better method to serve our vision. That's what makes a good tradition. It serves a godly purpose and can be changed as the Lord leads.

RUDIMENTS OF THE WORLD

The rudiments or basic principles of the world refer to the spiritual powers of antichrist that manipulate people unwittingly. The spirit of antichrist has been in the world for centuries (see 1 John 2:18; 4:3). It spoils immature, innocent believers who do not have a basic understanding of God's Word. Whether you realize it or not, each of us is either receiving from the Spirit of Christ or from the spirit of antichrist. According to *Merriam Webster Dictionary, antichrist* means "one who denies or opposes Christ." In the Greek, it means "an opponent of Messiah (G500). It's not just that his spirit opposes Christ, but is an opponent in its opposition to Christ. It is a counterfeit messiah, a substitute for the real Messiah. Antichrist offers a false good or compassion, a counterfeit love and kindness, replacing what God calls *good* with what man calls *good.* It is Satan disguising himself as *"an angel of light"* (2 Cor. 11:14). Satan doesn't deceive the masses with outright evil and darkness; he manifests as a savior clothed in compassion (a false, counterfeit compassion). He calls *evil good* and *good evil.* He puts darkness for light and light for darkness, bitter for sweet and sweet for bitter (see Isa. 5:20). This is the spirit we are fighting today in our culture. When someone calls sexual perversion love or sexual purity hate speech, that is the spirit of antichrist.

When someone calls sexual perversion love or sexual purity hate speech, that is the spirit of antichrist.

While everyone recognizes we are in a battle, we're not just in a battle between good and evil. We are in a battle between man's definition of good and God's definition of good. Man's definition of good independent of God and His Word is the spirit of antichrist. It is a perverted good, a counterfeit. A "good" that's only good for a few, a good that tries to stand in for Christ. God's definition of good is actually *good.* It's doesn't change with circumstance or time. It doesn't change person by person. It's truly equitable and just. This was original sin in the Garden when Adam and Eve thought they could know or discern good and evil without God. They thought good and evil could be known in disobedience to God. People are still eating of that tree today and it always leads to death (see Gen. 2:16-17).

Before Christ, our lives were manipulated by the rudiments of this world. We thought we were smart. We thought we were wise and in control. But we were actually blinded to the truth. *"But if our gospel be hid, it is hid to them that are lost: in whom the* ***god of this world*** *hath blinded the minds of them which believe not"* (2 Cor. 4:3-4 KJV). Then, the glorious light of the gospel shined on us. Jesus opened our eyes, and we were saved:

> *And you He made alive, who were dead in trespasses and sins, in which you once walked*

> *according to the course of this world,* ***according to the prince of the power of the air****, the spirit who now works in the sons of disobedience, among whom also we all once conducted ourselves in the lusts of our flesh, fulfilling the desires of the flesh and of the mind, and were by nature children of wrath, just as the others.*
>
> **Ephesians 2:1-3**

Wow! The same spirits that once blinded our minds and manipulated us are working in the world today, but we do not have to submit to them. We can instead submit to the rhythms of God's grace that guard our hearts from Satan's deadly poison. Satan does not have the power to spoil us and plunder our inheritance without our consent. Let's keep moving from faith to faith, glory to glory, and grace to grace as we work these disciplines into our lives.

Chapter Ten

KINGDOM FIRST

But seek ye first the kingdom of God, and his righteousness; and all these things shall be added unto you.

Matthew 6:33 (KJV)

We've talked about three things that help unload our hearts of fear and stress: taking heed to ourselves, resigning our messiah complex, and casting our care on the Lord. But the process of rest doesn't end there. You also must learn to refill your heart with the right things. Unloading the heart must now be reloaded with Kingdom principles.

Putting God's Kingdom first recalibrates our heart and clarifies our thinking. Jesus said, *"But seek ye first the kingdom of God, and his righteousness; and all these things shall be added unto you"* (Matt. 6:33 KJV). If we've been commanded to seek first God's Kingdom, then it's important for us to know what that Kingdom is. God's Kingdom is where He rules and reigns. It is where the Lordship of Jesus is honored and received. Like other kingdoms that have a king, Jesus is King of God's Kingdom. This is one of the few comparisons to God's Kingdom and the world.

God's Kingdom is different than the kingdoms of this world. It doesn't have boundaries or natural leaders. Earlier in Matthew 6:10, Jesus prayed for God's Kingdom to come and His will to be done on earth *"as it is in heaven."* He didn't pray that heaven would come to earth. He prayed that the earth would begin to look like heaven. Heaven is a place where God's Kingdom—His rule and reign—dwell, but it's not the only place it exists.

God's Kingdom exists anywhere Jesus—the King of that Kingdom—has the preeminence, anywhere He is Lord. Jesus said, *"The kingdom of God does not come with observation.... For indeed, the kingdom of God is within you"* (Luke 17:20–21). And Paul said, *"The kingdom of God is not eating and drinking"*—the Kingdom of God is not a matter of meat or drink (Rom. 4:17). In other words, it's not carnal or physical. God's Kingdom is His presence and goodness. It is *"righteousness and peace and joy in the Holy Spirit"* (Rom. 14:17). On earth, it exists in hearts submitted to Jesus. The Kingdom resides with the Holy Spirit in you and expands as His rule and reign of righteousness, peace, and joy, all working in our lives (see 1 Cor. 6:19).

God's Kingdom exists anywhere Jesus—the King of that Kingdom—has the preeminence, anywhere He is Lord.

So, what does it mean to seek God's Kingdom first? How do we get what's in our spirit into our daily lives? We place God's will first and foremost. We are loyal to Him above all else. And we realign our thoughts by setting them on God. Colossians 3:1-3 states,

> *If then you were raised with Christ, seek those things which are above, where Christ is, sitting at the right hand of God. Set your mind on things above, not on things on the earth. For you died, and your life is hidden with Christ in God.*

When your mind—your thoughts, will, and emotions—line up and agree with your spirit, what's in your spirit cannot help but flow out. It's like an irrigation ditch. The water in that ditch flows in whatever direction the ditch goes. As you realign your thoughts and set your mind on things above, the life force of the Kingdom flows through your soul and into your daily life.

By setting our minds on God and His promises and blessings, we displace worry and replace it with thoughts that build our faith. In Matthew 6:25 (KJV), Jesus told us to *"take no thought"* for our lives or bodies. Six different times He referred to our thoughts as they related to God's Kingdom. Don't worry about what we will eat, what we will drink, or what we will wear (see Matt. 6:25). And yet, worrying and "taking thought" about such things are how most people fill their minds. To truly experience life and peace, we must learn to *"take no thought"* and instead, "take God's thoughts" about our lives. That's what Christian meditation is all about. You cannot separate seeking God's Kingdom first independent of the thoughts we choose to take. Meditation is one of many disciplines that harness our thoughts, setting them on things above.

Some people associate meditation with Christian Science, but it's really just good Christian sense. Others think of meditation as "mind over matter." No, Christian meditation is a method of mind renewal that states how much your "mind matters." It is not like the Eastern philosophy of Transcendental Meditation ™ or the psychobabble of "becoming one" with the universe or God. In Christian meditation, we're not meditating to become one with God. Because of what Jesus did, we're already united to God (see 1 Cor. 6:17; Col. 1:27). We're not trying to overcome problems with our minds, but we recognize that our minds do matter. Christian meditation is how we set our minds *"on things above, not on things below"* (Col. 3:2). It's a lifestyle in which we think about God's promises and use those thoughts to counter every negative idea that pops into our brains. Christian meditation is the opposite of worry; it's a form of prayer (see Ps. 5:1-2). Worry is setting our minds on the things below.

The power of the Christian life doesn't come from the mind. But it does come through it. As we've discussed before, Romans 8:6 (KJV) declares, *"For to be carnally minded is death; but to be spiritually minded is life and peace."* As believers, we get to choose what our minds think on. We can think on carnal things—things associated with our five senses. Or we can think on spiritual things that are revealed in God's Word as truth and agreed upon by the Holy Spirit. When I seek what is righteous according to God's Word, pursue His kind of peace, and experience joy in the Holy Spirit, I am seeking His Kingdom first.

The power of the Christian life doesn't come from the mind. But it does come through it.

In my experience, two things typically cause believers to be carnally minded—to think on only earthly things, to consider what their flesh wants above what God is asking of them, and to be dominated by the pressures of this world. One is poor time management. The other is misplaced priorities. These things cause our hearts to become overloaded. They create unnecessary stress and lead to different forms of death.

TIME MANAGEMENT

In my early years, I struggled with time management. I knew people who worked thirty hours a week whose lives were extremely productive, while I was working sixty hours a week with very little to show for it. I didn't know how to use my time wisely. Time is our most valuable commodity. There is nothing more precious. We all have a limited amount of time, yet the same twenty-four hours in a day. And once it's spent, it is gone. We can't get it back. So, how do some people accomplish twice as much as others in the same amount of time? They've learned to *"walk circumspectly."* Being a good steward of time is essential to rest and peace.

> *See then that you walk circumspectly, not as fools but as wise, redeeming the time, because the days are evil. Therefore do not be unwise, but understand what the will of the Lord is.*
>
> **Ephesians 5:15-17**

Circumspectly means diligently. When we don't know God's basic will, we are not diligent. We do not spend our time wisely. Colossians 4:5 speaks of this same thing. It calls each of us to "redeem the time." According to *Strong's Concordance,* to redeem time is to buy it up, to ransom or rescue it from loss (*exaggerator,* G1805). Things unrelated to God's Kingdom rob us of time. Though sometimes necessary, too much time spent on these pursuits can render us unproductive and unfruitful. We buy back that time by seeking His Kingdom first and making God's will our priority. Time and focus on the wrong things take away time from the right things. Seeking the Kingdom first brings back time lost in trivial pursuits. There are many mysteries in God's Kingdom. One is time. When we seek His Kingdom first, we accomplish more in less time. When we quit seeking, there never seems to be enough time. An example of this is Israel worked six days a week and rested on the seventh. They accomplished more and were blessed above all the other nations who worked seven days a week. Putting God first brought more fruit in less time. Instead of losing a day, they increased productivity in six days. Seeking God's Kingdom and His will redeems time.

PRIORITIES

Priorities are also something else many people struggle to keep in order. For years, I didn't know what my priorities were supposed to be, much less recognize when they were out of order. But that's

Seeking God's Kingdom and His will redeems time.

what happens when you aren't managing time properly. Your priorities get all mixed up, and you start to crash. Often when people feel this way, they begin unloading their lives of all the wrong things. Like on a sinking ship, they panic and start unloading the things they need. They try to "buy back" time by ditching church or skipping Bible reading and prayer. When finances feel tight, they stop tithing.

If you're too busy or too stretched to do the things God asks of us in His Word, then you're too busy. Your priorities are out of order. Learn to unload the right things—your problems, worries, and cares—and hold on to the things that can help you. Hold on to the things of God. We must seek first His Kingdom, and trust that all those other things will be added to us as well. Our number-one priority must be God. That's what it means to make Him Lord. Nothing else works or even matters if we miss this. God's Word becomes final authority in the affairs of life and, therefore, a top priority in our lives. What does God say in His Word, which is His will?

During my senior year of college, I sensed a strong call of God on my life for ministry. I felt the Lord asking me if I was willing to lay down everything else to follow Him. At the time, I was pursuing a teaching and coaching career in tennis. Sue and I were in our first year of marriage, so being a good provider was on my mind, and it seemed as if things were going to work out. But after praying about it, both of us agreed it was time to move on. We were willing to follow the Lord wherever He led, even if that was away from a future in tennis. So, I laid down my racket, quit college, and asked the Lord, "What's next?" Suddenly, everything in my heart changed. My desire for tennis was gone. I didn't want to coach or teach.

God supernaturally unloaded all that to make room in my life for His will.

I went to Bible college. (The Lord had already been speaking to Sue about this as well, and when I asked her about it, she said she'd already prepared her resignation letter at work!) Sue and I packed everything we owned in a little trailer and pickup truck and headed to Oklahoma. It didn't really make sense, but like Abram, we were willing to leave everything behind and embark on this journey with the Lord. I am certainly not implying that this is how God speaks to everyone, nor is it something I would recommend to anyone who doesn't feel the Lord's prompting. But God was faithful to lead us through it, and He blessed our obedience.

When God and His will become our number-one priority, everything begins to fall into place.

I know we would not have heard His voice had we been carnally minded. That doesn't mean the only things we did were go to church or read our Bibles. That's not what it means to be spiritually minded (though those things can help). If, at that time, we were not seeking first His Kingdom and embracing the truths He was showing us about His love and promise to never leave or forsake us, we would have been too busy, our lives would have been too loud to hear His still small voice. But because our minds were fixed on Him, our lives were filled with His life and peace, and it was easy to discern His voice. When God and His will become our number-one priority, everything begins to fall into place.

PARABLES

When Jesus spoke to the multitudes, they had not developed this discipline of hearing God's voice. So, He used parables to give them a picture of how spiritual principles work. Several of His parables compared the Kingdom of God to seed (see Matt. 13). He said that the seed of God's Kingdom, His Word, is sown into the soil of our hearts. There, it either grows and produces a harvest or is choked out. The results depend on the soil of our hearts.

I choose to believe that your heart is good ground and my words are seeds of the Kingdom that will take root, and in time, bear fruit—*"some a hundredfold, some sixty, some thirty"* (Matt. 13:8). But according to Jesus' parables, I know I am not the only one sowing seed into your heart. The world is also sowing seeds, which the Bible calls "tares" or weeds. In Jesus' parable, when the man's servants discovered that his master's fields were growing both wheat and tares, he wanted to uproot the weeds. The master told them not to. *"...'Sir, did you not sow good seed in your field? How then does it have tares?' He said to them, 'An enemy has done this.' The servants said to him, 'Do you want us then to go and gather them up?' But he said, 'No, lest while you gather up the tares you also uproot the wheat with them. Let both grow together until the harvest, and at the time of harvest I will say to the reapers, 'First gather together the tares and bind them in bundles to burn them, but gather the wheat into my barn'"* (Matt. 13:27-30).

I love this parable. Jesus made it so clear that the Master was not the author of the weeds. He didn't sow the bad seed.

His enemy did. Jesus also made it clear that though both grow together for a time, a day will come when the reapers (His angels) will separate the tares from the wheat and cast them into the fire. Then the wheat will be gathered into God's house. Dear ones, God does allow good and evil to co-exist for a season. But a day of reckoning is coming. Evil will be purged. And His good seed, the children of the Kingdom, will be saved.

What many people don't realize is that while the seed of the Kingdom is in us, we are also Kingdom seed that God has planted in the field of our world. You matter. Your life counts. Regardless of how you feel or what your circumstances look like, God is using your life to testify of His Kingdom. You are making a difference. Be bold, take courage, and don't be afraid. Share your faith. Give your testimony. Tell the world who Jesus is and all He has done for you. Your life is like the mustard seed Jesus spoke of in Matthew 13:31-32.

> *Another parable He put forth to them, saying: "The kingdom of heaven is like a mustard seed, which a man took and sowed in his field, which indeed is the least of all the seeds; but when it is grown it is greater than the herbs and becomes a tree, so that the birds of the air come and nest in its branches."*

As a child of the Kingdom, you may feel small and insignificant like a mustard seed, but in reality, you are a tree of righteousness in which the world can find refuge. Through your life—or rather, God's life flowing through you—they find truth, light, and freedom. Your life, submitted to God, is like

As a child of the Kingdom, you may feel small and insignificant like a mustard seed, but in reality, you are a tree of righteousness in which the world can find refuge.

yeast working through bread dough. It progressively spreads though every part of your being and eventually makes its way out into the world (see Matt. 13:33).

In the New Living Translation of Matthew 13:33, Jesus said, "*The Kingdom of Heaven is like the yeast a woman used in making bread. Even though she put only a little yeast in three measures of flour, it permeated every part of the dough.*" I don't think it's by accident that this parable mentions yeast in three measures of flour. As human beings, we're made up of three parts—spirit, soul, and body (see 1 Thess. 5:23). Our spirit is where the Kingdom of God resides. But God's intention is for it to leaven our soul and body as well. From there, Kingdom leaven spreads to the whole world. We just need to learn to cooperate with it.

I know it may seem as though the leaven of the Kingdom isn't working. But it is. We're just the first generation to have constant access to the bad things happening all over the world. It can be overwhelming. But this world was a far darker place before Jesus came into it. For more than twenty centuries, Kingdom leaven has been working its way through our planet, and I believe we've got "the end of the world" backward. Many Christians seem to think things will only get worse before Jesus returns. They think light will get weaker and that darkness will overtake the world. Some even believe we should be building bomb shelters and stocking up on canned goods and weaponry so we can go into hiding when the antichrist comes. I don't believe that is a biblical perspective. Scripture is clear, *"Greater is he that is in* [us], *than he that is in the world"* (1 John 4:4 KJV). It also says, *"The path of the just is like the shining sun, that shines ever brighter unto the perfect day"* (Prov. 4:18). Things should be getting better and brighter as the day of the Lord approaches. We should be getting stronger and stronger as the Kingdom of God leavens us and starts leavening the world. I'm not saying there is no darkness or even gross darkness. I'm saying that while darkness is increasing, the light is as well. We are getting brighter in the darkness.

In Daniel 2, King Nebuchadnezzar had a terrifying dream of a tall statue divided into sections. In his dream, the statue, which seemed incredibly strong, was destroyed by a stone cut *"not by human hands"* (Dan. 2:34 NLT). The king called all his advisors in to learn the meaning of his dream, but only Daniel could interpret it. Daniel told the king that each section of the statue represented a different world kingdom. And during the reign of those kingdoms, another Kingdom would appear—one not made with human hands. The rule of that Kingdom would destroy all others until there was nothing left but dust. That Kingdom would then grow into a mountain covering the whole earth to *"never be destroyed or conquered"* (Dan. 2:36-44 NLT).

Perhaps that Kingdom is already here. Perhaps that rock has already hit the root of the kingdoms of this world. Perhaps they are already crumbling—beginning in our own lives.

Perhaps we need to reconsider our understanding of the "end times" and be open to changing our thinking about how God is working and moving in these last days.

Perhaps we need to reconsider our understanding of the "end times" and be open to changing our thinking about how God is working and moving in these last days. People all over the world are being saved. And those who know the Lord are beginning to act like it. God is doing something huge in this generation, and as we cooperate with it, His Kingdom will affect us spirit, soul, body, and world. We who believe in Christ overcome the world, God wins, and Satan loses. While sin and darkness abound, grace and light abound more (see Rom. 5:20).

Chapter Eleven

A LIVING SACRIFICE

I beseech you therefore, brethren, by the mercies of God, that you present your bodies a living sacrifice, holy, acceptable to God, which is your reasonable service. And do not be conformed to this world; but be transformed by the renewing of your mind.

Romans 12:1-2

Two things are essential in the transformational, leavening process of the Kingdom—offering our bodies to God as living sacrifices and renewing our minds. A living sacrifice is not a one-time sacrifice. It is a continual act of faith, a continual "coming unto Jesus." And though it can be painful to sacrifice our old ways of thinking and doing, we must stay on the altar. We must put the old ways of self-love, self-effort, and self-sufficiency to death by grace and the power of the Holy Spirit.

Much of the sacrifice we experience in this life is achieved by the denying of self as a disciplined follower of Christ (see Matt. 16:24). But this loss of self is the key to living well in God's Kingdom. It requires humility and a dependence on Christ that accepts the truth that "without Jesus I can do nothing" but since I am never without Jesus, *"I can do all things through Christ who strengthens me"* (John 15:5; Phil. 4:13). And while being a living sacrifice implies a certain level of suffering, it is suffering God calls us to by His grace and tender mercy, not wrath or fear of punishment.

THE DEATH OF THOUGHT

Jesus said in John 12:24, *"Unless a grain of wheat falls into the ground and dies, it remains alone; but if it dies, it produces much grain."* Have you sacrificed your old life and thoughts since coming to Jesus? As we discussed previously, thoughts—both good and bad—are like seeds. In time, these seeds will bring forth a harvest, and so dear ones, if you don't like your harvest, look to your seed. Are you proud of your "progressive" thoughts about marriage, love, and sexual purity? Are you allowing your opinions and beliefs to be shaped by culture instead of God's Word? If so, you are planting a bad seed, the seed of independence from God. You need to humble yourself and allow that seed to die. Plant the seed of God's Word, and you will begin to see the change you desire.

I see this often. As I share the seed of God's Word, I see people's thoughts and opinions on the altar of their minds. But more often than not, people don't allow for the death of their old beliefs. They don't become a living sacrifice. They do not realize there is no lasting change without mind renewal. Their five senses (sight, taste, hearing, smell, and touch) dominate their way of thinking or discerning good and evil. They are led by emotions rather than the Holy Spirit. A living sacrifice is when we trust God's Word above our senses and *"walk by faith, not by sight"* (2 Cor. 5:7).

Romans 12:2 tells us not to *"be conformed to this world, but be transformed by the renewing of"* our minds. The word *conformed* here means to be "poured into the mold of; shaped like, look like; to fashion like or after the same pattern" (*suschamatizo*, G4964). Why do so many Christians look and sound like the world? They have not suffered the pain of becoming a living sacrifice. They have not allowed the godly sorrow of their unrighteous thoughts to lead to repentance. And instead of changing their minds, they have allowed their thoughts to be shaped by the world.

The word *renewed* in these verses from Romans means "to renovate" (*anakainosis*, G342). If you've ever renovated a house or piece of furniture (or seen one on TV), you know that before the restoration process can begin, demolition has to occur. An antique chair must be stripped and sanded before a new finish can be applied. Our old thoughts must also be stripped away before our new thoughts can bring about transformation. There must be a demolition of the old worldly way of thinking to make way for the renovation of the mind to cause transformation of our lives. That's a painful process called *"a living sacrifice."* This explains why the Church at large is so worldly and locked into immaturity and offense. Being a living sacrifice is

Why do so many Christians look and sound like the world? They have not suffered the pain of becoming a living sacrifice.

not a popular concept. Forsaking our unrighteous thoughts can be a major part of being a living sacrifice (see Isa. 55:7).

The Greek word for *transformed* here is *metamorphoo* (G3339). This is the same word we get our English word *metamorphosis* from—the radical changing of the structure of an animal by a supernatural means, as in the change from a caterpillar to a butterfly. Unfortunately, many Christians never experience the beauty and freedom of metamorphosis because they refuse to repent and become a living sacrifice.

I once addressed the evils of partial-birth abortion in one of my sermons, and a woman got up to furiously storm out of the church. I spoke to her later and was surprised when she admitted to being offended that I would publicly say such things. She knew abortion was wrong. She knew it grieved God's heart. But she was more offended by my public rebuke of such an evil than she was the act of abortion itself. Addressing the problem was more appalling than the sin itself. People like this will vote for people that support such a crime against humanity.

I wonder, if I lived in the 1860s and preached about the evils of slavery and value of human life, would that too have been deemed "inappropriate" by her standards? Or if I lived in Germany in 1935 and spoke out about the evils of the Nazi regime, would she find that offensive as well? (And please understand, I am using this woman as a stand-in for the American church at large. I am not singling her out, specifically.) She was at least honest with me when I spoke to her. Many in the Body of Christ have similar worldviews. Their thoughts and actions have been shaped and conformed to the world's standard. They have not become a living sacrifice. When we suffer persecution and afflictions and false accusations for righteousness, we are a living sacrifice.

PERSECUTION

Psalm 4:5 says, *"Offer the sacrifice of righteousness, and put your trust in the Lord."* In some settings, doing the right thing can cost you. Just speaking the truth in love can bring persecution or rejection. Sometimes, doing the right thing can even be more costly, demanding a sacrifice. Many are being sued for righteousness' sake in our culture of darkness and unrighteousness. Others have lost their jobs following a righteous conviction over the institution of marriage, pursuing sexual purity, or even vaccine mandates.

Sometimes, doing the right thing can even be more costly, demanding a sacrifice.

The apostle Paul dealt with this concept of letting go of the old to embrace the new when he wrote to the church at Philippi. He said it was the "one thing" he did to facilitate Kingdom change in his life.

> *This one thing I do, forgetting those things which are behind, and reaching forth unto those things which are before, I press toward the mark for the prize of the high calling of God in Christ Jesus.*
>
> Philippians 3:13-14 (KJV)

I believe the mark Paul spoke of is our high calling of being conformed into the image of Jesus. That is our predestination (see Rom. 8:29). It's our mark of maturity (see Eph. 4:13). It's *"Christ being formed in"* us (Gal. 4:19). Christlikeness is how we experience the fullness of God's Kingdom. And it is accomplished in this *"one thing."* We must forget our old way of thinking, forget our old way of living (both the mistakes and successes), and reach toward this new way of dependence on God. We must press into the things of God no matter what obstacles we face or opposition we experience. We have to become a living sacrifice. The pressing can be painful as the opposition can come from the least expected places. I know that when I was young, pressing into God's plans for my life brought opposition from my own family and friends. It was painful.

We must be willing to be rejected by the world and receive honor that comes from God only. Jesus said in John 5:44, *"How can you believe, who receive honor from one another, and do not seek the honor that comes from only God?"* We must die to the fear of man as well as seeking the world's honor (see Prov. 29:25). The biggest enemy of faith is caring what others say or think of you. We need to care what God says or thinks.

Only by utilizing these three elements in tandem—forgetting, reaching forward, and pressing through—can the "one thing" be achieved. We cannot forget if we do not reach for the good God has for us. And we will not obtain if we do not press through. Quit looking in your rearview mirror. Stop thinking back and rehearsing your losses. Look forward. Fill your thoughts with His goodness and goodwill for your life.

Give yourself permission to dream with Him. And press into all God has for you and your family. That is the one thing.

The *forgetting* Paul talked about is not a type of spiritual amnesia or memory loss. Rather, it is a choice to not think on past things with regret or guilt. Paul never forgot the bad things he did before his Damascus encounter with Jesus (see Acts 9). He often testified of how God changed him from a persecutor of the Church to an apostle. So, he did look back on his life. But he looked back through a redemptive eye. He refused to let his past mistakes define his present reality in Christ. He refused to allow guilt and condemnation to sabotage his future. He "forgot" by letting go of the shame and reaching toward God's good will for Him in Christ. He refused to give up on God's redemptive plan and pressed through Kingdom opposition. He kept his windshield-view (every new "in-Christ reality" he experienced) in the forefront. And he allowed the rearview of his past to stay where it belonged—in the past.

Abraham demonstrated this powerful truth of leaving behind the old and pressing toward the new when he left his homeland to follow God's voice. Hebrews 11:10 (NIV) declares that Abraham sought for a country *"whose architect and builder is God."* He was so focused on that goal that he became immune to the temptation to return. Abraham refused to look back. *"And truly, if they had been mindful of that country from whence they came out, they might have had opportunity to*

Paul refused to let his past mistakes define his present reality in Christ.

have returned" (Heb. 11:15 KJV). Looking back, what the world calls "leaving your options open," gives place to temptation. It leaves the tiny seed of "other" (which can be anything "other" than what God said) to grow in your heart and mind. But Satan can't tempt you if there is no "other" option.

Sue and I have been happily married for over four decades. A major key to our success is the decision we made not to let divorce be an option in our relationship. Refusing to give thought to something, like divorce, closes the door on fulfilling that thought. We repented of the worldly philosophy of "finding Mr. or Mrs. Right" and embraced God's philosophy on marriage. (And I can tell you, when you don't have a Plan B, you work really hard to make Plan A successful!)

Romans 12:2 (KJV) goes on to say that when we do become living sacrifices and renew our minds, we *"prove what is that good, and acceptable, and perfect, will of God."* That is, we experience a transformed life. Every time we repent—every time we change our minds and choose to stop thinking like, sounding like, and acting like the world, and start thinking like, sounding like, and acting like Jesus—we prove this process. We adjust our thoughts from a "secular worldview" to a "biblical worldview" and experience transformation.

HARDSHIPS

Many Christians wrongly assume that trials and tribulations also bring about this transformation. Nothing could be further from the truth. Trials do not mature us. But responding to them as a living sacrifice does. Trials and tribulations test our faith. And James 1:2-6 instructed us how to pass that test with an A+.

> *My brethren, count it all joy when you fall into various trials, knowing that the testing of your faith produces patience. But let patience have its perfect work, that you may be perfect and complete, lacking nothing. If any of you lacks wisdom, let him ask of God, who gives to all liberally and without reproach, and it will be given to him. But let him ask in faith, with no doubting.*

This verse is so applicable to our daily walks with the Lord. God wants to give us wisdom in every trial, every persecution, and He wants to reveal His love and faithfulness to us. But if we don't know how to relate to problems properly, we'll get off the altar and short-circuit our transformation. James said the first step in relating properly to our problems is to *"count it all joy."*

Joy is not usually an emotion associated with trials or hardship. But joy is an act of faith in the midst of them. As we *"count it all joy,"* James said that *"the testing of* [our] *faith produces patience."* And that patience helps us mature in Christ. Think about that. Believers who relate properly to trouble don't just *go* through hardship; they *grow*

If we don't know how to relate to problems properly, we'll get off the altar and short-circuit our transformation.

through it. Faith and patience produce the character of Christ in our lives to the point that we *"lack nothing."* Wow! James said we need to "know this," not feel it. Our joy is in knowing God's faithfulness in our trials, and faith and patience produce maturity of character.

Submitting to God (which is an act of faith) and resisting the devil (which is patience) develop our character. They're like lifting weights. You can fill your home with free weights, bar weights, and other workout equipment, but if you never use them, those weights will not help you build muscle mass. You have to "resist" the weights—lifting, curling, and pressing them over and over—to produce that change. Trials do not perfect you. If they did, we would all be perfect because we all have them. They do not help you mature into Christlikeness. Responding properly to trials through faith and patience perfects you. People who do not respond in faith and patience become bitter. Those of us who do respond in faith and patience become better.

Romans 5 makes this same point. *"We also glory in tribulations,* ***knowing that*** *tribulation produces* ***perseverance*** [or patience]; *and perseverance, character; and character, hope"* (Rom. 5:3-4). Notice again how joy, amid suffering, is not connected with what we feel. It comes out of what we know. We have to know that by staying on the altar of a living sacrifice and responding properly to our trials, we will develop patience, and patience will produce Christlike character in our lives. And in that knowing, we can find joy just like the apostle Paul.

Therefore we do not lose heart. Even though our outward man is perishing, yet the inward man is being renewed day by day. For our light affliction, which is but for a moment, is working for us a far more exceeding and eternal weight of glory, while we do not look at the things which are seen, but at the things which are not seen. For the things which are seen are temporary, but the things which are not seen are eternal.

2 Corinthians 4:16-18

PEANUT BUTTER

How we feel in a trial is temporal. What we believe is eternal. Feelings change and vacillate; God and His Word never change. This is how I learned the power of thanksgiving. Thanksgiving is the sound of faith. It's how we *"count it all joy."* Years ago, when my children were in school, we lived 25 minutes from town. My oldest daughter was a real talker, so all I had to do was ask, "How was your day?" and she'd fill those 25 minutes to the brim. One day, when my daughter was about six, instead of telling me about her day, she sang me a song (this is her version). "Peanut sittin' on a railroad track, his heart was full of butter. He didn't hear the 516...Choo! Choo! Peanut butter." It was just a silly kid song, but I knew there had to be a point in there somewhere, so I asked her to sing it again. She did, and it struck me that whatever your heart is full of, comes out when trials hit. Jesus said in Matt. 12:34, *"Out of the abundance of the heart the mouth speaks."*

Whatever your heart is full of, comes out when trials hit.

If your heart is set on being a living sacrifice, when the trials and tribulations of life appear, joy will come out. First Thessalonians 5:18 says, *"In everything give thanks; for this is the will of God in Christ Jesus for you."* Notice it doesn't say *"for"* everything give thanks. We don't thank God for evil or things contrary to His will. However, we do thank Him in it. We don't thank God for our problems; we thank Him for His faithfulness in them and for our deliverance. We thank Him in trials that patience is being produced in our lives, and we are developing character. We count it all joy. We thank Him that *"through faith and patience we inherit the promises"* (Heb. 6:12).

Years ago, after teaching on this concept a person approached me after the service to correct me over my interpretation of Scripture. This individual believed we were to thank God *for* all things instead of *in* all things. I asked what Scripture they based this belief on, and they responded with Ephesians 5:20 (KJV) which says, *"Giving thanks always for all things unto God and the Father in the name of our Lord Jesus Christ."* I tried to explain that this Scripture was not saying to thank God *for* all things, but rather to always give thanks for all things *unto God*. The phrase *"unto God"* matters. God doesn't want praise for things that He is not a party to. I do not thank God for evil, Satan, sin and its effects on humanity and their hearts. They weren't satisfied with my answer but let me try to explain.

Jesus was once approached by the Herodians with a question about taxes. They wanted to trap Him into answering unlawfully—they didn't care about the truth or the law; it was meant to entrap him.

> *Tell us therefore, What thinkest thou? Is it lawful to give tribute unto Caesar, or not? But Jesus perceived their wickedness, and said, Why tempt ye me, ye hypocrites? Shew me the tribute money. And they brought unto him a penny. And he saith unto them, Whose is this image and superscription? They say unto him, Caesar's. Then saith he unto them, Render therefore* ***unto Caesar*** *the things which are Caesar's; and* ***unto God*** *the things that are God's.*
>
> Matthew 22:17-21 KJV

Jesus' point: The Kingdom of God and the kingdoms of this world are separate. God doesn't want praise for the evil of this world. He doesn't want praise for what bears Satan's image. He doesn't want praise for anything with Satan's fingerprints on it. (Satan's fingerprints, Jesus said in John 10:10, are stealing, killing, and destroying.) He went on to declare He came to "give us life" and that we may have it more abundantly. God wants praise and thanksgiving for the things that bear His image. He desires for us to give thanks *in* everything, knowing that He is working everything together for our good and growth into Christlikeness. He doesn't ask us to give thanks *for* everything. I don't thank God for cancer and the horrors it creates. I thank Him in it for my healing and deliverance.

I've heard it said, "It can't get any worse," regarding Jonah. As bad as it was in the belly of a fish, it could have been worse. There were two ends to that fish! Things could have gotten worse!

Part of being a living sacrifice is praising and thanking God in everything regardless of how we feel. Regarding our new condition in Christ, Peter puts it this way: Christ being the Chief Corner Stone, we also, *"as living stones, are being built up a spiritual house, a holy priesthood, to offer up* ***spiritual sacrifices*** *acceptable to God through Jesus Christ"* (1 Pet. 2:5). Thanksgiving is one of those sacrifices we offer in faith to God in the trials and tribulations of life. Psalm 116:17 (KJV) speaks of *"the sacrifice of thanksgiving."* My favorite out of all Scripture is Jonah in the belly of the fish in Jonah 2:9 (KJV), *"But I will sacrifice unto thee with the voice of thanksgiving...."* I've heard it said, "It can't get any worse," regarding Jonah. As bad as it was in the belly of a fish, it could have been worse. There were two ends to that fish! Things could have gotten worse! You get my point. (Let it go). In the darkest place thought possible, Jonah offered the sacrifice of praise. God turned it all around and worked both His will for Jonah and Nineveh as well. It all started with Jonah being a living sacrifice and offering thanksgiving in all things.

Chapter Twelve

FAITH FOR THE JOURNEY

For we walk by faith, not by sight.

2 Corinthians 5:7

God has called each of us to walk and live by faith. Faith is the antidote to worry and fear. It is our "no fear zone." Paul encouraged a young pastor, Timothy, to find this place of peace and refuge in God by fighting the good fight of faith. *"Fight the good fight of faith, lay hold on eternal life, to which you were called and have confessed the good confession in the presence of many witnesses"* (1 Tim. 6:12).

Faith, dear ones, is a fight. It's a fight within ourselves to believe God and His Word regardless of our circumstances or sense of unworthiness. It's a fight to believe that God is good amid a culture of death. And it's a fight to believe that our faith in Jesus and the power of the gospel is not misplaced when we see all the evil and corruption around us. But that faith is a good fight. It's good because—if we don't give up and renounce our "good confession"—we win. We will see the manifestation of our hope (see Heb. 10:23; 11:1). We will see the results of our faith. We must mix faith with God's Word and promises in order to benefit from them. The promise of rest in Scripture must be mixed with faith as well (see Heb. 4:2).

Romans 5:1-2 says, *"Therefore, having been justified by faith, we have peace with God through our Lord Jesus Christ, through whom also we have access by faith* ***into this grace*** *in which we stand, and rejoice in the hope of the glory of God."* These rhythms of grace are accessed by faith. We need God's grace that has abounded toward us, and we must mix faith with that grace to prosper. We need grace and faith. It is God's grace that makes faith a good fight.

No one calls a fight "good" if they lose. I only had one good fight as a kid. I've been part of several others (not because I initiated them, but I got dragged into them anyway), but they were not good. One nearly killed me. If it hadn't been for my brother pulling the kid off me, I might have died. (It was not a good fight!) On another occasion a fight presented itself, I determined I was not going to lose. I would die before admitting defeat. I kicked. I scratched. I bit and fought like a girl all the way to victory. It was a good fight. Still, she nearly beat me! (Let it go.)

The lessons I learned from that one good fight have served me well to this day. We have to fight the way God called us to fight. We don't fight with people. That's a recipe for disaster. We don't even fight to obtain the things God has promised us in His Word. Rather, we fight to maintain our good confession. We fight to protect what has already been obtained for us by grace. We fight against our flesh to enter into the complete, finished work of Christ on the cross. The author of Hebrews calls this fight the *"labour ... to enter into that rest"* (Heb. 4:11

KJV). That same chapter in verse three declares, *"...we which have believed do enter into rest...."*

We also fight against principalities and powers in spiritual warfare, knowing that we can experience victory in and through Christ Jesus our Lord. Paul talked more about this spiritual fight and the weapons God has provided for us in Ephesians 6. One piece of the six is said to be of most importance:

> *Above all, taking the shield of* ***faith*** *with which you will be able to quench all the fiery darts of the wicked one.*
>
> Ephesians 6:16

Of all the weapons God has provided for successful warfare, faith is the most vital. Faith is a currency of the Kingdom. It is how we please God and must be mixed with every other spiritual principle or weapon for that principle or weapon to be of benefit to us (see Heb. 4:2; 11:6). Faith is also a shield. It quenches all of Satan's darts and protects us from worry, anxiety, and fear. Faith provides light to our spiritual eyes and allows us to walk in God's Kingdom principles. It makes us effective with the other five weapons (girdle of truth, breastplate of righteousness, gospel of peace, helmet of salvation, and sword of the Spirit or Word of God).

Of all the weapons God has provided for successful warfare, faith is the most vital.

> *The lamp of the body is the eye. If therefore your eye is good, your whole body will be full of light. But if your eye is bad, your whole body will be full of darkness. If therefore the light that is in you is darkness, how great is that darkness!*
>
> Matthew 6:22-23

What we focus on will dominate our hearts and lives. Fear has a focus as does faith. Fear focuses on lies, fraud, and darkness. Faith focuses on truth, transparency, and light. God has called us out of darkness unto His Kingdom of light. Through Christ, we are called to be light (see Matt. 5:14; Eph. 5:8).

There is no greater darkness than a child of light, a Christian, continuing to live in darkness. When we value the world's system above God's Kingdom, we become party to the death, deception, and darkness that are in the world. If COVID-19 taught me anything, it is that Christians, at large, are as carnal and fearful as the world. God gave me a clear word regarding COVID-19 and the mandates that would come out of it. He told me not to fear, but to boldly stand for freedom, the right to work, and the sovereignty of our bodies as the temple of the Holy Spirit. I was canceled by more than one social media platform over that. But even now, when I try to expose all the fraud and lies ensnaring this generation, I get as much pushback from Christians as from media hacks and propagandists. What great darkness has befallen the Church!

Twitter and Facebook were not the first to conceal truth. Cancel culture started in the Church. In many circles the truth is rejected as much as in any place in the world. I'm not saying this to condemn anyone, but unless we wake up, the soft tyranny of corrupt government systems will not cease. Election fraud will continue, and we will descend into a country oppressed by dictators. All the things we are dealing with now—weaponizing science for political gain, weaponizing our government institutions (i.e., FBI and IRS), and an out-of-control media—will continue and escalate until people are held accountable. The good news is we are in the beginning stage of a great awakening. Light is shining in dark places, with sin and corruption being exposed. God's people are waking up and turning back to Him, His Kingdom, and His righteousness. Prodigals are coming home. The lost are fleeing Egypt and turning to God. The Kingdom is advancing because the just are choosing to live by faith (see Matt. 11:12; Gal. 3:11).

Romans 10:17 says, *"So then faith comes by hearing, and hearing by the word of God."* Faith begins and ends where God's Word is known. It comes by hearing (which is characterized by listening and obeying) God's Word and is fed the same way. Fear comes from listening to the world, and it too must be fed. Neither faith nor fear can survive without fuel. The world supplies fear's fuel through lies, fraud, and vain philosophies. Feeding on those things will produce fear and worry in your heart. But if you feed on the gospel (the good news of who Jesus is and what He accomplished on the cross to make you and me sons and daughters of God and co-heirs with Him), it will produce faith.

Faith begins and ends where God's Word is known.

Colossians 2:6-7 says, *"As you therefore have received Christ Jesus the Lord, so walk in Him, rooted and built up in Him and established in the faith, as you have been taught, abounding in it with thanksgiving."* Just like we received Jesus as Lord by grace through faith, we walk in Him by grace through faith. Remember, grace is what God does for us independent of ourselves. Faith is our positive response to that grace. We must choose to believe, to be "rooted and built up in Him" so we can be established in the faith. And we must be disciplined to keep hearing the Word of God and, in humility, accept it as final authority.

So, how does this faith work? By Kingdom laws or principles that show the eternal truth and constant nature of God's Word. Romans 3:27 says, *"Where is boasting then?"* In other words, if we are saved by grace through faith, there is no place for boasting. *"It is excluded. By what law? Of works? No, but by the* ***law of faith****."* Notice faith is a law and is governed by spiritual laws. Just like there are certain principles and laws that govern the world God made, so there are spiritual laws that govern the Kingdom. These laws are constant and were created to be a blessing to us when we understand and cooperate with them. Consider the law of gravity. Without gravity, life on this planet would be impossible. The law of gravity is a blessing. But if that law is violated, if you jump off a building, what was created to be a blessing will become the antithesis of one. This truth is hidden all over creation—the laws of motion (which include inertia, momentum, and aerodynamics), the law of thermodynamics (energy), and the laws of electricity.

Do you know the laws of aerodynamics were around in Jesus' day? People could have flown airplanes in biblical times had those laws been discovered. We (meaning people in the twenty-first century) didn't invent aerodynamics, the laws of thrust and lift that override the law of gravity. The only reason we have airplanes today is because someone discovered the laws that govern motion and thrust, and we benefited from them. The same is true for electricity. The laws that governed electricity existed in the Garden of Eden. Adam and Eve could have had artificial light had they known of those laws. How many more natural laws are waiting to be discovered? What inventions (benefits) might those laws inspire?

Kingdom laws also have to be discovered and cooperated with in order for us to benefit from them. I grew exponentially when I realized this truth. When I learned the laws governing faith—like how it comes and what it sounds like—my prayer life exploded. So did my fruit. I realized that, up to that point, I'd been complaining instead of praying, walking in doubt and unbelief instead of faith. The fruit of my life wasn't reflecting what I saw in Scripture because I didn't understand grace and faith. I was trying to earn God's blessings and favor instead of simply receiving it by faith. God, in grace and by grace, had already provided everything I needed at the cross. All He required out of me was to believe and receive. I learned how faith speaks and my words were either death or life, fear or faith.

Proverbs 18:21 says, "*Death and life are in the power of the tongue, and those who love it will eat its fruit.*" And Jesus said in Matthew 12:34, "*For out of the abundance of the heart the mouth speaks.*" We are eating the fruit of our lips. To this day, I meet Christians who

I was trying to earn God's blessings and favor instead of simply receiving it by faith.

do not understand the power of our words and how faith works. They mock any teaching from Scripture as it relates to words, not realizing they are mocking faith and the laws that govern faith. I couldn't go on speaking words of doubt and defeat and expect the fruits of righteousness to grow in my life. Second Corinthians 4:13 says, *"And since we have the same spirit of faith, according to what is written, 'I believed and therefore spoke,' we also believe and therefore* ***speak****."* Fear speaks, and faith speaks. Fear speaks in murmuring and complaining. Faith speaks in praise and thanksgiving. Faith is eternally optimistic for it knows in whom it has believed (see 2 Tim. 1:12). When trials come to separate us from God, faith speaks: "God is for me. He loves me, and nothing can separate me from His love. I'm going to make it through this" (see Rom. 8:37-39). Faith addresses the obstacles of life with an attitude of victory (see Mark 11:23-24). It speaks to the mountain as Jesus taught us to do. Fear, on the other hand, lets those mountains talk to you and convince you that God is not able (or willing) to help, especially you!

Let me share with you some of the unchangeable laws of faith that I've learned. These cooperative powers work with our faith similar to the way an atom works in nature. If you remember from science class, an atom is the building block of matter. It's the source of nuclear energy and is made up of a nucleus which contains neutrons, protons, and electrons.

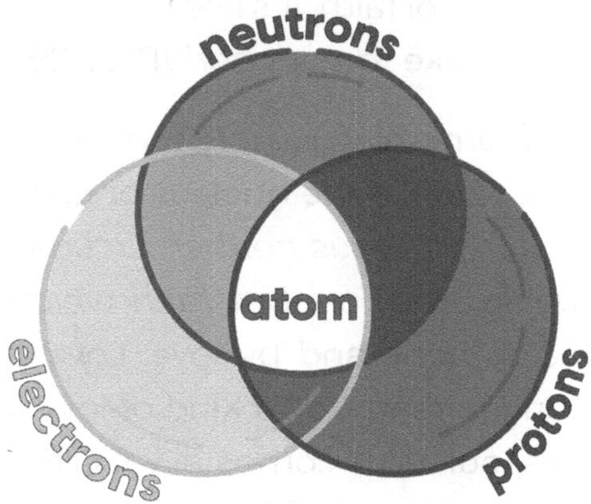

Each of these particles has an electric charge that, together, determines the mass and energy of a particular element (atom).

Faith, too, has a nucleus. And within that nucleus, the three cooperative powers of hope, love, and patience give substance to a power that can move mountains.

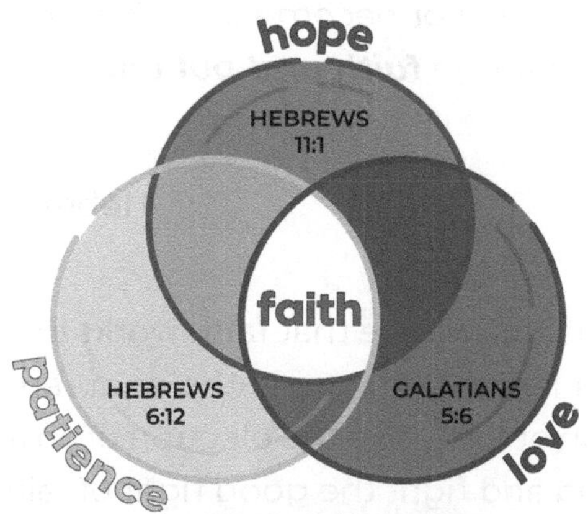

Hebrews 11:1 says: *"Now faith is the substance of things* ***hoped for****, the evidence of things not seen."* Faith works in

hope. Hope is the vision of faith. It's like the neutron of an atom and grounds our faith like *"an anchor"* (Prov. 29:18; Heb. 6:19).

Hope gives faith something to hold on to, but like the atom, hope does not rest alone in the nucleus of faith. Galatians 5:6 (KJV) says, *"For in Christ Jesus neither circumcision availeth any thing, nor uncircumcision; but faith which* ***worketh by love****."* Faith works in hope and by love. Love is the spirit of faith. When we understand God's kind of love and know the love He has for us, our faith comes alive. Like the proton of an atom, love binds the Word of God in our minds and writes it on our hearts (see Prov. 3:3). It pushes out what doesn't belong to faith and attracts the third element necessary to see the manifestation our faith come to pass—patience (see 1 John 4:18).

> *And we desire that each one of you show the same diligence to the full assurance of hope until the end, that you do not become sluggish, but imitate those who through* ***faith and patience*** *inherit the promises.*
>
> Hebrews 6:11-12

And so, my friends, we see that faith works in hope, by love, and through patience. Patience is the endurance of faith. It may seem like an outlier—like the electron of an atom—but as we learn to stand and fight the good fight of faith, we experience the faithfulness of God for ourselves (see Heb. 10:23). This produces thanksgiving and develops within us the confident steadfastness we need to keep walking by faith even when we don't see results as quickly as we'd like. When each of these elements work in tandem, they create a positive, explosive power that can move mountains (see Matt. 17:20)!

Chapter Thirteen

COOPERATIVE POWERS OF FAITH

Where is boasting then? It is excluded. By what law? Of works? No, but by the law of faith.

Romans 3:27

Faith is described here as a law, a governing principle in God's Kingdom. There are spiritual laws that work with our faith, making us world overcomers. The AMPC translation of Romans 3:27 calls faith *"a principle."* Let's look deeper into each of faith's cooperative powers that are spiritual laws and principles of faith.

HOPE

Hebrews 11:1 states, *"Now faith is the substance of things hoped for, the evidence of things not seen."* Hope comes first in our lives, and faith brings substance to those hopes. Hope is future tense, and faith is now. We've talked a lot about hope throughout this book, but according to *Strong's*

Concordance, biblical hope means "to perceive; to see, anticipate with pleasure; confidence" (*elpois,* G1680). Hope is the vision of our faith; without it we simply perish (see Prov. 29:18).

Satan understands the vital role hope plays in our faith. That's why he attacks it so relentlessly. Hope inspires. It keeps us dreaming and imagining a good future, a future worth living for. You and I can go forty days without food, three days without water. But we cannot live a single day without hope. Hope works with faith like a thermostat works with an air-conditioning unit. Alone, a thermostat has no power to cool a house. The AC unit outside has the power to cool, but without the thermostat, the potential energy of that unit sits idle with no way for us to access its power. The unit itself gives substance to whatever temperature the thermostat sets and can keep the indoor temperature at a comfortable 72 degrees. Can you see how vital hope is to our faith? The thermostat of hope serves as the goal, dream, or vision that ignites the power unit of faith, bringing substance to our hopes.

The faith of the Christian life is built on the *"blessed hope"* revealed in First John:

> *Behold what manner of love the Father has bestowed on us, that we should be called children of God! Therefore the world does not know us, because it did not know*

You and I can go forty days without food, three days without water. But we cannot live a single day without hope.

> *Him. Beloved, now we are children of God; and it has not yet been revealed what we shall be, but we know that when He is revealed, we shall be like Him, for we shall see Him as He is. And everyone who has this* ***hope*** *in Him* ***purifies*** *himself, just as He is pure.*
>
> **1 John 3:1-3**

But this blessed hope is not just in the return of our Lord. It is that we will be like Him. Hope purifies us and directs us toward holiness in our lives. It inspires us to keep moving forward. As believers, we put our hope in the resurrection, in Christ's return, and in the redemption of our bodies (see John 14:1-4; Rom. 8:23; 1 Cor. 15). We hope in God's promise of a new heaven and new earth without darkness or evil (see Rev. 21). And this hope keeps us stable through the storms of life (see Heb. 6:19).

Romans 15:4 says, "*For whatever things were written before were written for our learning, that we through the patience and comfort of the Scriptures might have* ***hope***." Like faith, hope comes from the Scriptures. Receiving God's Word creates hope and gives faith something to bring substance to. Get your hopes up! Envision the promises of God coming to pass in your life. Don't let Satan steal your hope. Don't let the world kill your vision. Allow yourself to dream. Love others but avoid intimate fellowship with hope snatchers, vision assassins, and dream killers. Without hope, your faith will have nothing to aim at. Never lose hope in the promises of God, even when you may be wavering in your faith.

LOVE

Faith is the byproduct of God's love for you. As Galatians 5:6 (KJV) says, *"For in Christ Jesus neither circumcision availeth any thing, nor uncircumcision; but faith which **worketh by love.**"* But there is so much confusion over what love is that people often struggle to recognize God's love. Today, people speak of love as desire, anticipation, pleasure, or a virus that comes and goes. You hear about people falling in and out of love. It comes and goes like there is no control over it. They use the term to describe so many things it has become descriptive of nothing. "I love ice cream." "I just love this weather." "I love my dog." "I love my wife." But the love you have for your wife should be different than the love you have for your dog. (And that doesn't mean you can prefer your dog over your wife!) With so many different definitions for the word love, it's no wonder people don't understand what it means when we say, "God loves you."

With so many different definitions for the word love, it's no wonder people don't understand what it means when we say, "God loves you."

We need a revelation of true love—God's kind of love—so that our faith can work. We need to understand God's love for us so it can destroy the spirit of fear in our lives. But how do we know God loves us? How do we discern His love personally? Paul's prayer for the church at Ephesus may help. He prayed,

> *That Christ may dwell in your hearts through faith; that you, being rooted and grounded in love, may be able to comprehend with all the saints what is the width and length and depth and height—to know the love of Christ which* ***passes knowledge****; that you may be filled with all the fullness of God.*
>
> **Ephesians 3:17-19**

Wow! God's love is limitless. His love is so great it *"passes knowledge."* This tiny phrase is important to grasp. How can you know something that passes knowledge? Only by revelation.

Knowledge that comes from God and His Word supersedes knowledge that comes from our carnal minds and physical senses. We can't discern God's love by our circumstances. We can't know it by feelings. Romans 5:5 (KJV) declares that God's love *"is shed abroad in our hearts by the Holy Spirit."* The Holy Spirit reveals God's love to us and causes the fullness of Christ to be seen and known in our lives. Even our maturity into Christlikeness is connected to knowing God's love in a way that *"passes knowledge."* After knowing love by revelation, Paul declared *"that we might be filled with the fulness of God."* God's love brings transformation by faith into Christlikeness.

The passage of Scripture below describes four revelations of God's love that you and I need to understand.

> *Beloved, let us love one another, for* ***love is of God****; and everyone who loves is* ***born of God and knows God****. He who does not love does not know God, for*

> ***God is love.*** *In this the love of God was manifested toward us, that God has sent His only begotten Son into the world, that we might live through Him.* ***In this is love****, not that we loved God, but that He loved us and sent His Son to be the* ***propitiation for our sins****.*
>
> 1 John 4:7-10

GOD IS LOVE

These revelations touch on the length, depth, width, and height of God's love. The first is that *"God is love"* (vs. 8). Love is God's nature and personhood. Love is who He is, not just what He has. If you "love" your dog, that love can be measured and contained. You can have more or less of it depending on your dog's behavior. But if you *are* love, there is no measurement attached. You simply are. Look at water as an example. If you have a pitcher of water, you can measure it—one cup, two cups, a liter, a drop. You can give more water to one family member and less to another. But if you are H_2O, you are the same to every member of your family. Now it's up to them to choose how much water they will use and what they will use it for. One might use a cup of water to get a drink. Another might use several gallons to do the laundry. Someone else could fill a swimming

Love is God's nature and personhood. Love is who He is, not just what He has.

pool and have a party—the supply (at least for the purpose of this illustration) is limitless.

That's what God's love is like. Love is not just what He has for you; it's who He is. That's how His love can be unconditional. We are the ones who love conditionally. We are the ones who accept others based on their performance. We are the ones who use phrases like, "I love you thi-i-i-is much," and "I love you more." God just says, "I love you." And since love is who He is, not a response to what we do, His love is unmerited and is the same to us all. There is nothing good you can do to get Him to love you more nor anything bad to get Him to love you less. That's how He can love us all the same. Believe it or not, God's love for you is equivalent to the love He has for Jesus! Jesus was praying for us in John 17 and made a profound statement regarding God's love.

> *That they may be made perfect in one, and that the world may know that You have sent Me, and have loved* ***them as You have loved Me****.*
>
> **John 17:23**

Wow! Let that sink in. The love God has for you is the same love He has for Jesus. No wonder faith works by love. My faith is soaring as I write this!

LOVE IS OF GOD

The second revelation of love from 1 John 4:7 is that *"love is of God."* It comes from Him and Him alone. Love is not of this world. It's not of our flesh or circumstances. That's why the world does not know what true love is. That's why we can't depend on our feelings to tell us whether or not we are loved. Love is not a physical, carnal emotion. When the world tries to define love outside of God, or when religion tries to describe God outside of love, they lie. You cannot separate love from God or God from love.

First Corinthians 13 defines love as patient and kind; not envious, boastful, or proud; not rude or self-seeking; not easily angered. It says love keeps no record of wrongs. It doesn't *celebrate evil* but *rejoices in truth*. It protects, trusts, hopes, and perseveres through every circumstance. Love never gives up. Notice that none of those character traits are based on feel-good emotions. There is no lust or sexual perversion listed among them. Nothing we can fall into or out of. Love is not selfish. It doesn't divorce your wife because of a blonde, Cambodian-refugee-look-alike. It doesn't fulfill sexual desire with a child or explore fantasies with someone of the same sex. Not one trait listed in 1 Corinthians reflects the world's definition of "love." Because as Romans 13:10

No matter how much one believes what they are experiencing is motivated by "love," if it causes harm or is selfish, it is not love. And it is not of God.

(KJV) tells us, *"Love worketh no ill to his neighbour."* God's love doesn't harm others. Child molestation harms. Homosexuality harms. Fornication harms. Adultery harms. No matter how much one believes what they are experiencing is motivated by "love," if it causes harm or is selfish, it is not love. And it is not of God.

BORN AGAIN AND KNOW GOD

Thirdly, we must be born of God and know God to love with His kind of love (see 1 John 4:7). People who are not born again cannot love with God's kind of love. Even people who are born again can miss it if they don't know that God is love or what His love looks like (see 1 Cor. 13).

Immature Christians who haven't come to truly know God often believe something that God condemns is love. *"He that loveth not* ***knoweth*** *not God, for God is love"* (1 John 4:8 KJV). When we condone what God condemns, we are not reflecting love. Until we come to know God, we cannot love one another with His kind of love. The best we can do is produce a cheap counterfeit.

In Romans 12:9 we read, *"Let love be without dissimulation. Abhor that which is evil; cleave to that which is good."* Dissimulation means hypocrisy. When we come to know God and His kind of love we understand how evil destroys the human heart and people's lives. Sin gives Satan place in our lives, and he will steal, kill, and destroy (see John 10:10; Rom. 6:16). It hurts us and all those around us. It is God's love for us and others that wants to see people free from sin and all its consequences. It is God's love in our hearts that wants to see God's best for everyone (see Rom. 5:5). It's in my walk with Jesus that I've come to hate evil because I see the pain and misery sin creates. I've come to cleave to good and experience the blessing it brings to myself and others. Again, 1 Corinthians 13:6 says that God's love *"does not rejoice in iniquity, but rejoices in the truth."*

THE CROSS

The last revelation of love is the cross. Thankfully, Jesus showed us love so we wouldn't be confused. He was love made flesh (see John 1:14; 1 John 4:9). And that love was revealed at the cross: *"**In this** the love of God was manifested toward us, that God has sent His only begotten Son into the world, that we might live through Him. **In this** is love, not that we loved God, but that He loved us and sent His Son to be the propitiation for our sins"* (1 John 4:9-10). *Propitiation* means satisfaction. Jesus died to satisfy *"the righteous requirement of the law"* (Rom. 8:3-4). He paid the penalty for our sins, and in so doing manifested or showed the love of God to the whole world.

We did not initiate God's love. We didn't love God first and He then reciprocated that love. No, God loved us, and Christ died for us *"while we were still sinners"* (Rom. 5:8). We were not lovely or worthy of any good thing from God. We were actually unlovely. The cross and sacrifice of Jesus for our sins forever proves God's love for us.

God's love for you is the same as His love for Jesus.

Earlier, I said that God's love for you is the same as His love for Jesus. I understand how hard that is to imagine. At one time, we were all enemies of God (see Rom. 5:10). Jesus was perfect. He never fell short—not in word, thought, or deed! Of course, God loves Him. But how could God love me as much as Jesus when I have sinned and fallen short of His good plan countless times? Dear one, those thoughts are just a holdover of your unrenewed mind. You're thinking of love in terms of performance. God's love is based on Who He is. Not what you have or have not done. He is Who He is to us all. His love is based on His character, not my conduct whether good or bad. His love was an action (the cross), not an emotion.

If God loved Jesus more than you, why would He send Jesus to pay for your sins? Why wouldn't He make you pay for them? Jesus' sacrifice on the cross reveals just how much God loves us. Only God's kind of love would be so selfless. Only real love would make such an offer.

We did not initiate or deserve God's love. We couldn't earn it or pay it back. That's what we mean when we say God's love is unconditional. Romans 5:8 says, *"But God demonstrated His love toward us in that while we were still sinners, Christ died for us."* God loved us when we were still sinners, when we ignored Him and treated Him as the enemy. When all we did was to fulfill our own lusts, the love of God came. It was shed abroad in our hearts by the Holy Spirit. And it took the Holy Spirit's work to reveal that love to us. As believers, it still takes the Holy Spirit to reveal the depths of God's love so that our faith can work.

PATIENCE

Hebrews 6:12 says, *"that you do not become sluggish, but imitate those who through faith and patience inherit the promises."* It's not by faith alone we inherit all of God's promises; it is though faith and patience. The last power connected to faith is patience. Patience is the strength and endurance of faith.

As children of God, we are called to walk by faith and run our race with patience (see 2 Cor. 5:7; Heb. 12:1). Unfortunately, many in the Body of Christ don't consider the importance of patience. Preachers don't talk about it, and believers try to avoid it. They have viewed faith as a shield to protect them from problems—in the sense of never having any—instead of the strength to endure problems. But the very definition of patience is "longanimity that is forbearance or fortitude: longsuffering" (*makrothumia*, G3115). It also means "cheerful endurance" (G5281). "Bearing pains or trials calmly or without complaint" is how the *Merriam Webster Dictionary* defines patience. This word puts to rest the myths about great faith meaning problem-avoidance; neither does "great faith" exempt us from trials and hardship. As Christians, we should expect opposition to our faith. But developing patience will allow our faith to work during opposition.

Chapter Fourteen

KINGDOM OPPOSITION

And from the time John the Baptist began preaching until now, the Kingdom of Heaven has been forcefully advancing, and violent people are attacking it.

Matthew 11:12 (NLT)

One thing modern-day believers have forgotten is that the Bible paints the blessings and benefits of knowing Christ against a backdrop of Christian suffering. They misunderstand what the *"life and peace"* promised in Romans 8:6 means. They think it is a promise that they won't ever experience opposition or hardships in this life. But that's not true. Even about prosperity Mark 10:29-30 says, *"There is no one who has left house or brothers or sisters or father or mother or wife or children or lands for my sake and the gospel's who shall not receive a hundredfold now* ***in this time****—houses and brothers and sisters and children and lands,* ***with persecutions****—and in the age to come, eternal life."* It's all right there, in the same Scripture. Our promised hundredfold return of all we have sown for the gospel's sake comes with a backdrop of persecution. Unfortunately, much of the persecution will come from other members of the body of Christ. Yet how many Christians want the blessing of prosperity but are unwilling to endure its persecution? God never promised a trouble-free life to those who enter His Kingdom, but He did promise that we could have a trouble-free heart (see John 14:1; 16:33; 2 Tim. 3:12).

Our promised hundredfold return of all we have sown for the gospel's sake comes with a backdrop of persecution.

Colossians 1:13 says, *"God has delivered us from the power of darkness and conveyed us into the kingdom of the Son of His love."* Scripture is clear. We've been delivered from the *power* of darkness, but we have not yet been delivered from the *presence* of darkness. This world is a dark place. But we should not be intimidated by the prince of the air or any "power" he wields. We've been delivered from his influence.

Second Timothy 3:12 says, *"All who desire to live godly in Christ Jesus will suffer persecution."* There is opposition to God's Kingdom in this life, and that opposition must be met with resolve as we *"stand against"* the powers of darkness clothed in God's armor (Eph. 6:10-12). However, too many Christians do not put on the full armor of God and live clothed in the *"armor of light"* (Rom. 13:12). They are not prepared for the persecutions and afflictions that come by seeking God's Kingdom first. While there are different levels and forms of persecution that come with living godly, we all experience persecution for righteousness in an unrighteous world. It may be subtle like being mocked or defriended on social media for sharing scripture, but could be as severe as prosecution and then in some countries execution.

For years, I thought that if I lived a good moral life, people would accept me. Everyone would speak well of me and love me; life would be good. But Jesus lived a good moral life. He obeyed God perfectly, and they crucified Him. Jesus was God made flesh, yet He was hated, reviled, mocked, rejected, and despised. If that's the way the world treated Love on Earth, why do we think the world will treat His ambassadors any differently?

Jesus was God (love) made flesh, and the world that claims to love totally rejects Love. While they demand tolerance in the name of so-called love, they have no tolerance for God's kind of love or the God who is love (see 1 John 4:8).

In John 17:14, Jesus said, *"I have given them Your word; and the world has* ***hated them*** *because they are not of the world, just as I am not of the world."* And again, in Matthew 10:22, He said, *"And you will be* ***hated*** *by all for my name's sake, but he who endures to the end will be saved."* Those who belong to God's Kingdom will be rejected by this world. Persecution is actually a witness to your relationship with Jesus. John 15:18-19 says, *"If the world* ***hates you****, you know that it* ***hated Me*** *before it* ***hated you****. If you were of the world, the world would love its own. Yet because you are not of the world, but I chose you out of the world, therefore the world* ***hates you****."* Believers who don't understand this truth will never become disciples. Persecution will turn them away. The pressure of affliction will overload their hearts.

No one likes rejection. We were created for acceptance. But when we know how loved and accepted we are by God, man's rejection means nothing (see Ps. 118:6). God loves us. He is for us and has accepted us in His beloved—Jesus (see Rom. 8:31; Eph. 1:6). Who cares what other men say? God's love is enough. His acceptance is all we need. The apostle Paul understood this. Even after being persecuted, severely beaten, stoned, and left for dead, Paul returned to the cities where those things occurred to encourage the disciples who lived there. He told them to not be surprised by trouble, but to remain strong in their faith.

> *And when they had preached the gospel to that city, and had taught many, they [Paul and Barnabas] returned again to Lystra, and to Iconium, and Antioch, confirming the souls of the disciples, and exhorting them to continue in the faith, and that we must through* ***much tribulation enter into the kingdom of God****.*
>
> Acts 14:21-22 (KJV)

When we know how loved and accepted we are by God, man's rejection means nothing.

This is what Jesus taught them and us if we will be humble and receive it. In John 16:33, Jesus said, "*These things I have spoken to you, that in Me you may have peace. In the world* ***you will have tribulation;*** *but be of good cheer, I have overcome the world.*" You will have tribulation, not may have, or perhaps have. It is as expected and natural as getting wet in the rain.

Converts don't like this. They may see the Kingdom, but it takes discipleship—submitting to God's Word—to enter and experience the Kingdom (see John 3:3; 8:31-32). And that discipleship will be met with afflictions, persecutions, and tribulations from this world. That's why we see so few Christians step up, stand up, or speak up for truth. They're afraid. They are afraid and intimidated by the opposition that comes with the morals and principles of the Kingdom, and when confronted, they back up. They go silent. Instead of seeing persecution as a blessing and proof that they love God, they fear man's response. They dread the social pressure and price they may be called to pay.

They seek the praise of men rather than of God. They please men rather than have faith in God's Word and please God. *"Nevertheless among the chief rulers also many believed on him; but because of the Pharisees they did not confess him, lest they should be put out of the synagogue: for they* ***loved the praise of men*** *more than the praise of God"* (John 12:42-43 KJV). People refuse to act in faith on God's Word because they desire the praise of the world. They fear the rejection of man and it becomes a snare (see Prov. 29:25). Now I know many do not believe God praises us or is ever pleased with us, but He does and is. If you don't understand God's love for you, you will never be delivered from an unhealthy need for man's love and acceptance.

In Matthew 5:10 Jesus declared, *"Blessed are those who are persecuted for righteousness' sake, for theirs is the kingdom of heaven."* Notice the connection with the Kingdom and opposition. In the next two verses, Jesus unpacked this blessing further. *"Blessed are you when they revile and persecute you, and say all kinds of evil against you falsely for My sake. Rejoice and be exceedingly glad, for great is your reward in heaven, for so they persecuted the prophets who were before you"* (Matthew 5:11-12). Jesus promised that when we endure persecution for His name's sake, we are in the prophet class, and are blessed, both on earth and in heaven. Rejoice and be exceedingly glad? The source of this type of rejoicing and gladness comes from the promise of rewards in heaven. It took me a while to discipline my emotions in persecutions, to acting in my faith in God's promise of rewards.

Early in ministry, I wasn't prepared for persecution. I thought, if I did a good job sharing the Word, everyone would say, "Good preaching, little preacher." Boy was I naïve. I remember ministering one Sunday, years ago while in the Methodist Church, about being one in Christ and how that unity changes who we are and how we see one another. As I taught on this new identity in Christ (one of my favorite subjects!) and how God sees us as His children regardless of our background, gender, or race, I read these verses in Galatians:

Jesus promised that when we endure persecution for His name's sake, we are in the prophet class, and are blessed, both on earth and in heaven.

> *For ye are all the children of God by faith in Christ Jesus. For as many of you as have been baptized into Christ*

> *have put on Christ. There is neither Jew nor Greek, [here I added the phrase "Black or White"] there is neither bond nor free, there is neither male nor female: for ye are all one in Christ Jesus. And if ye be Christ's, then are ye Abraham's seed, and heirs according to the promise.*
>
> Galatians 3:26-29 (KJV)

After the service, I moved to the back door as I always did, to shake hands and visit the people. Everything seemed to be going well until a man stepped up to me with his fists clenched. His eyes shot daggers at me, and his words were just as sharp. He called me all sorts of names (not all of which were accurate) and slung words around that should never be repeated. I could tell that he really wanted to hit me, but something seemed to be holding him back. (I believe it was an angel. And since his arms were as big as my thighs, I was grateful. He could have really hurt me!) I'm not exactly sure how long this exchange lasted, or even what made him leave, but after I got home, I headed straight to my office to pray. Actually, I was crying out. "How could I make someone so mad? What did I do to stir up such hatred?" I felt so bad. Then, one of the deacons of that church called to "exhort" me to be careful what I said and how I said it. It was not a loving rebuke or one of encouragement. It was more of a hint that I better be more careful and not upset anyone in the congregation.

As I sat there wallowing in self-pity, my dear, loving wife walked by. She stopped at my door and said, "What's wrong with you, Big Man of Faith and Power?"

To say I didn't appreciate being jarred out of my pity party would be an understatement. I gave Sue all kinds of reasons to justify my behavior. I had a right to be upset! I had a right to have my pity party even if Satan was the only one attending.

Sue didn't agree. "Are you going to let a little persecution keep you from ministering the Word of God?" It felt like a slap in the face. But then she began exhorting me in a much different way than the deacon had. She told me how powerful the message was and what a good job I'd done explaining how much God loves us and desires to live through us—how God had totally reconciled us back to Him and now with one another. There is no place for racial discrimination in the heart of a Christian. Period. We are all family and now one in Christ. Then Sue told me that if I hadn't done such a good job, the devil wouldn't have been so upset. She encouraged me to get used to persecution because it always came to those who refused to compromise God's Word.

I later learned that the man who attacked me was a former member of a local Ku Klux Klan (KKK). I know what true white supremacy looks like, sounds like, and acts like. I'd stirred up the racist spirit within him by confronting it with the Word. Racism is a matter of sin, not skin. It doesn't care what "color" heart it hides or abides in. Whether it be the KKK, critical race theory, Black Lives Matter Inc., Nazism, or any other philosophy, it's all the same spirit, and I will never be intimidated by it again. God's Word and truth confront it, expose it, and expel it.

Racism is a matter of sin, not skin.

God used my wife to help me get my eyes off myself and allow God to heal that hurt before it took root in my heart. She confirmed the call of God on my life and encouraged me to strengthen myself in the grace and peace of our Lord Jesus Christ. She reminded me to come unto Jesus and learn of Him. And amid that persecution, I learned to take man's criticism to the feet of Jesus and allow Him to correct my missteps. As much as I care about people and want to help them, I cannot be a man-pleaser (Prov. 29:25).

Jesus said in Luke 6:26, *"Woe to you when all men speak well of you, for so did their fathers to the false prophets."* A lack of persecution for my messages and everyone speaking well of me would put me in the false prophet class. I certainly don't want that. Sometimes it is our enemies that best define who we are.

Jesus made a profound statement in John 5:44, *"How can you believe, who receive honor from one another, and do not seek the honor that comes only from God?"* We can't fear man. Caring about what others think more than what God thinks kills Bible faith. We have to esteem God's Word and put faith in what He says, or fear will eat us up.

In this life, we will suffer persecution. We don't get a pass. We are partakers in Christ's suffering. (In Philippians 3:10-11, Paul called it *"suffering with Christ"* and prayed that he would *"know him, and the power of his resurrection and the* ***fellowship of his sufferings****, being made conformable unto his death, if, by any means, I may attain unto the resurrection of the dead."*) Persecution is designed by Satan to derail our faith. He uses it to produce fear so he can steal God's Word from our heart (see Mark 4:16-17). So how do we keep from being overwhelmed in them? We learn to come to Jesus, remain yoked up to Him, and learn of Him in every circumstance. And we *"reckon that the sufferings of this present time are not worthy to be compared with the glory which shall be revealed in us"* (Rom. 8:18 KJV).

There is a blessing associated with persecution, a level of fellowship with Jesus that is not available through any other means. And while it's never God's will for us to be stressed, He does want us to be stretched. Relating properly to the hardships of life stretches and enlarges us, which in turn expands God's Kingdom.

Paul boldly preached the gospel and faced lots of opposition—from false accusations to beatings and shipwrecks to stoning and imprisonment. But he called each one a "light affliction." How could he do that? By *"counting it all joy."* Paul recognized that his afflictions were working in him a *"far more exceeding and eternal weight of glory."* (See 2 Corinthians 4:17). He looked beyond what he felt and saw in the moment of persecution to what he couldn't see—God's Kingdom advancing and the reward of the next life. We must do the same. When we respond to affliction and hardship in faith, *"Christ in us, the hope of glory"* begins to work its way out and we see God's will accomplished (Rom. 8:29; Col. 1:27). Our focus must remain on the unseen Kingdom of God.

While it's never God's will for us to be stressed, He does want us to be stretched.

Years ago, a romantic streak hit me, and I decided to do something special for Sue. She likes fireplaces, so I put a small wood-burning stove in our bedroom. I even cut a hole in the roof myself. I was so excited when it all came together. I had purchased three-pound, presoaked logs. It was time to light the fire even as the romantic fires were already inflamed. But being from Florida, I had no idea how presoaked logs worked. I put a log in the stove and lit it only to be disappointed in the fire it produced. So, against my wife's advice (She's from Indiana. What did she know about fires?), I added another and again reached in to light it. Suddenly, we had a fire! Flames shot out of the stove toward the ceiling. Smoke filled the room. I felt a sense of panic come over me while my adoring wife started laughing.

I was not a happy camper! What could possibly be funny about burning down the house?! I grabbed the closest liquid I could find to try and get the fire under control. Have you ever felt like you were charging hell with a water pistol? With the little spray bottle I use on my hair, that's exactly what I felt like. *Spritz. Spritz.* The fine mist of water that bottle put out did absolutely no good. So, I tried to beat the fire down. I grabbed the poker from our fireplace tool set and started beating the logs apart. (I can nearly hear the gasps, as I'm writing, from those of you who understand presoaked logs.) Instead of reducing the flames, all my beating accomplished was to give that fire more oxygen and ignite the fluid in those logs. By now, flames were coming out of the stove, and we had a much hotter fire than our bedroom needed or that little stove could handle. Eventually, Sue got herself under control and came up behind me with a big pitcher of water. *Whoosh!* The fire was out, and so was my romance.

The Lord showed me something in the fireplace debacle. He reminded me of Exodus 1:12 which says about the children of Israel, *"The more they afflicted them, the more they multiplied and grew."* At this time in history, Israel had been made slaves in Egypt. They worked under grueling conditions to build Pharaoh's cities and keep his fields, yet God was faithful to them. The more the Egyptians afflicted the Israelites, the more they multiplied and grew—just like my fire and the joy we should experience in Christ. When Satan strikes us with "light afflictions," God's glory within us is ignited. We multiply and grow in character and Christlikeness. And when we see how patience works with our faith, we are able to endure. Keep submitting to God's rhythms of grace in life's challenges, and God will work it all together for your good.

Chapter Fifteen

SPIRITUAL DISCIPLINES

And beside this, giving all diligence,
add to your faith virtue; and to virtue
knowledge; and to knowledge temperance;
and to temperance, patience....

2 Peter 1:5-6 KJV

Before diving into more spiritual disciplines that can help you overcome fear and live in the freedom and blessing God desires, it's important that you understand that grace—while opposed to legalism—is not opposed to discipline and diligence (see Titus 2:11-12). Grace is opposed to earning relationship or some other blessing from God. It's also important to understand that each of us are walking through different seasons of life, and sometimes those seasons influence how these disciplines work. The principle behind the discipline doesn't change, but the rhythm has to. That's why it's called a "rhythm of grace" and is part of what the Scripture means when it says we are to *"work out"* our own salvation (Phil. 2:12). The Holy Spirit works with us to develop rhythms of grace that fit each of our seasons of life and help us grow into mature Christ-followers.

When Sue and I had four children at home, I often planned ministry travel to limit the disruption to family time and school schedules my absence created. So, I would take the boys with me on one trip and the girls on another. During that season, having morning quiet time as husband and wife was not a reasonable rhythm. Today, it is. Our children are grown, and Sue and I travel together. Now we can start each morning with prayer, fellowship, and coffee. Coffee comes before prayer and fellowship improving the quality of both. We've developed that rhythm of grace around the principle of fellowshipping with God and each other. Together, we work out our salvation by discussing what God is saying to each of us, what we need to pray for, and the direction God is leading us in ministry and family.

Each of us needs to develop our own grace-rhythms around the daily disciplines of exposure to and study of Scripture, prayer and beholding God's glory, humility, maintaining godly relationships, and thanksgiving, just to mention a few.

STUDY OF SCRIPTURE

Psalm 119:11 (KJV) says, *"Thy word have I hid in mine heart, that I might not sin against thee."* God's Word is essential in the guarding and gardening of our hearts. It leads and guides us as we choose to yield to its authority (see Ps. 119:105; Isa. 30:21). But many in the Body of Christ are scripturally illiterate. We all need to find our own

Each of us needs to develop our own grace-rhythms.

grace rhythm of spending time with Jesus in the Scriptures. It's how we come to know Him.

God speaks to us and guides us in the challenges of life through the reading of His Word. *"All Scripture is given by inspiration of God, and is profitable for doctrine, for reproof, for correction, for instruction in righteousness, that the man of God may be complete, thoroughly equipped for every good work"* (2 Tim. 3:16-17). God corrects us out of His Word. He instructs us in good and evil and how to discern. He equips us to serve Him and one another as well as mature us in the process. We need to spend time with Jesus in His Word. God's Word is like food to our spirit man and spiritual growth (see Matt. 4:4; 1 Pet. 2:2).

Some people read the Bible from cover to cover every year. That is a great spiritual discipline and very beneficial to your spiritual growth and maturity. It was reading God's Word that healed me of dyslexia. *"To not let them* [God's words] *depart from your eyes; keep them in the midst of your heart; for they are life to those who find them, and* ***health*** *to all their flesh"* (Prov. 4:21-22). The Bible may have been my first book I read from cover to cover. That's how powerful God's Word is in our lives. I've read the Bible from cover to cover (even through the maps) several times, but I don't do it every year. I prefer to read passages and take time to meditate on them. This helps me receive understanding from the Word and retain what the Holy Spirit speaks to me. God may lead you to feed on His Word in a different way, but that way will also lead to life.

Second Timothy 2:15 (KJV) says, *"Study to shew thyself approved unto God, a workman that needeth not to be ashamed, rightly dividing the word of truth."* It is vital that we take time to read God's Word, hear it from anointed speakers, and meditate on it. For while everything in the Christian life begins with, "What does the Bible say about that," it is even more important that we discover, "What does the Bible mean about that, and how can I apply that to my life?" Bible study is a discipline that contributes to "rightly dividing" God's Word. It starts by recognizing the difference between Old and New Testaments (law versus grace) and develops into an understanding of types and shadows versus their substance in Christ.

Proverbs 1:2-3 (KJV) says the Scripture exists *"to know wisdom and instruction; to perceive the words of understanding; to receive the instruction of wisdom, justice, and judgment, and equity."* Scripture gives *"subtilty* [or prudence] *to the simple, to the young man knowledge and discretion. A wise man will hear, and will increase learning; and a man of understanding shall attain unto wise counsel"* (Prov. 1:4-5 KJV). And to those who heed its counsel, Scripture becomes a *"crown of grace"* for your head and a *"chain of honor"* for your neck (Prov. 1:9 NLT).

God's Word is the Word of grace, the gospel of good news (see Acts 20:24, 32). Studying God's Word reveals that grace to us and instructs us in His wisdom (see Prov. 4:13). We begin with knowledge— "what does God say?" We then get understanding— "what does God mean?" And the wisdom— "how does this apply?"

PRAYER

Prayer is another rhythm we need to develop in order to renew our minds and be conformed into the image of Christ. Now, when I say "prayer," I'm talking about all the ways we commune and communicate with God. Prayer can take on many forms. Meditation is a form of prayer. In Psalm 5:1-2 David said, *"Give ear to my words, O Lord, consider my meditation. Give heed to the voice of my cry, my King and my God, for to You I will pray."* Notice how meditation and prayer are used interchangeably in this passage.

"Being still" before the Lord is another important component of prayer. *"Be still, and know that I am God: I will be exalted among the heathen, I will be exalted in the earth"* (Ps. 46:10 KJV). It takes discipline to be quiet and listen for God's still small voice. It takes discipline to "be still" and "wait upon the Lord" so that we can come to know Him (Isa. 40:31). Being still is not a work of the law to get God to speak; rather it is an act of faith obedience. Being still tunes our hearts to hear what He is saying.

Prayer is all the ways we commune and communicate with God.

There are many other kinds of prayer—prayers of agreement (Matt. 18:19); prayers of petition (Phil. 4:6); thanksgiving (Ps. 100:4); prayer of faith (James 5:15); and praying in the spirit (Jude 1:20) just to name a few—and we should take time to learn them all. I have more teachings on prayer to assist you with this discipline, which you are welcome to download for free from my website. The most important thing to know about prayer is that prayer is rooted in relationship. Prayer helps us develop intimacy with God and is ultimately how we minister to one another. Prayer is how God has purposed to bring what God's will is in heaven to the earth (Matt. 6:9-10).

GOD'S GLORY

As we develop grace rhythms around God's Word and prayer, mixing faith with what we read and hear, we behold God's glory and see change in our lives. Second Corinthians 3:18 (KJV) says, *"But we all, with open face beholding as in a glass* ***the glory of the Lord, are changed*** *into the same image from glory to glory, even as by the Spirit of the Lord."* I'm not changed by beholding my glory. (I'm not changed by beholding my sin either.) I can't even be changed by listening to anointed preaching alone. Anointed preaching can inspire and encourage me toward change, but lasting change comes from beholding God's glory for myself.

Paul said, *"Do you have faith? Have it to yourself before God"* (Rom. 14:22). This does not mean our faith should not be publicly expressed. But it does mean our faith is based on a personal relationship with God. We can't impose faith on others, nor rely on others to establish our faith. We can only partner with them in faith. They must behold His glory.

We can't impose faith on others, nor rely on others to establish our faith. We can only partner with them in faith. They must behold His glory.

No matter how well I preach (or write) about the revelations God's given me, I can't change you. Only God can change your heart. Only He can convict, convince, and convert you, and He does that supernaturally as we behold His glory. It's a progressive, effortless change from *"glory to glory by the spirit of the Lord."* Now when I say effortless, I'm not saying we don't have to apply ourselves, or that there are no disciplines required. But lasting, positive change happens as we look to Jesus and trust His grace. We don't change for God—that would give us the glory. God changes us for Himself, from the inside out, and He receives all the glory. So what is God's glory?

This is what Jesus came to reveal. *"And the Word was made flesh, and dwelt among us, and we* ***beheld His glory*** *the glory as of the only begotten of the Father, full of grace and truth"* (John 1:14). Jesus revealed God's glory—His true nature and personhood. The glory of God is the true nature of God and His love and mercy. Beholding God's glory is what transforms us. It's supernatural and from within, Christ in us the hope of glory.

HUMILITY

As we take the time to behold God's glory, we develop trust in His love and care. We seek His wisdom and learn to cast our cares on Him. And we take the first steps toward walking in humility. I've already taught an entire chapter on humility, but this subject is worthy of review and further explanation.

Worry and self-effort are pride. They draw on the wisdom and strength of the flesh instead of relying on God. Each of us needs to develop rhythms around humility so that we can maintain a sober mind and heart. By centering our lives around Christ, we remind ourselves Who is ultimately in charge. We thank God for watching over us and praise Him for our many blessings while casting the care of our problems on Him because He cares for us. Humility opens the floodgates of grace (James 4:6).

But humility also involves submission and yielding to one another.

> *Likewise you younger people, submit yourselves to your elders. Yes, all of you be submissive to one another, and be clothed with humility, for "God resists the proud, but gives grace to the humble." Therefore humble yourselves under the mighty hand of God, that He may exalt you in due time.*
>
> 1 Peter 5:5-6

When we truly learn to submit to God, we also learn to submit to one another, and in that humility, we discover a grace to help us in our time of need. Part of God's grace toward you and me is found in other believers (1 Pet. 4:10). That's why being part of a community of faith is so important. We limit God's power in our lives when we try to live in isolation.

We limit God's power in our lives when we try to live in isolation.

How many times have you thought, "I don't need help," or "I'll figure it out on my own"? That's pride. Proverbs 11:14 says, *"Where there is no counsel, the people fall; but in the multitude of counselors there is safety."* We tend to mess up when we refuse to seek help or receive from other believers and ministry gifts. We get ahead of ourselves. We miss an obvious (or not so obvious) answer. We hurt others. No one likes other people to know when we're dealing with problems, much less the specific nature of those problems. I get that! But embarrassment is just pride blushing, and everyone feels it at some time or another. "What will they think of me?" "What will others say?" That's pride, and it leads to destruction (Prov. 16:18). That leads me to the importance of mature, godly relationships.

GODLY RELATIONSHIPS

We all need check stations in life to help us through these times. We need people who can become places of refuge. And while these people never take the place of relationship with God, they can help us process hardship and unload the cares of this life onto God. If, for example, I have a ministry situation I can't seem to release, I humble myself and seek my wife's help. I don't come home and dump everything that happens in the ministry on her. But I do recognize that she is my co-laborer in Christ and a vehicle of God's grace in my life.

Peter declared us as being *"heirs together of the grace of life"* (1 Pet. 3:7). I trust her to encourage me in my faith and give me godly counsel when needed. So, I process the situation with her. If I still need help, I humble myself and go to one of my elders or spiritual friends. I explain the situation to them and ask for help. We pray together, and they offer advice as the Holy Spirit directs. Over the years, I've been amazed at how godly relationships have helped me process the worries and cares of ministry and life in general. Ultimately, each relationship has pointed me back to Christ and given me reason to rejoice in His amazing grace.

All of us need these encouraging, godly relationships to aid in our spiritual formation. Whether they be pastors, elders, or other spiritual leaders, these people provide a place of refuge and godly counsel when we need it. As a leader in the Body, the grace of God in me causes me to be a blessing to others. And as a member of that same Body, the grace of God in others blesses me when I humble myself to receive.

The grace of God in others blesses me when I humble myself to receive.

THANKSGIVING

Because we belong to God, joy resides in our spirits no matter what is happening around us (see Rom. 14:17). But to experience that joy on the outside, we must choose to rejoice. Philippians 4:4 says, *"Rejoice in the Lord always. Again I say, rejoice!"* Rejoicing doesn't necessarily mean singing and dancing (though there is nothing wrong with that); it is a decision to be thankful and choose joy. According to *Strong's Concordance, rejoicing* is a "calm happiness" (G5463). It's a positive attitude that has nothing to do with personality traits or brain chemistry. As we walk by faith and develop disciplines that constantly point us back to grace, we find a strength in the Lord that comes through rejoicing (see Neh. 8:10).

Philippians 4:5-9 (KJV) says:

> *Let your moderation be known unto all men. The Lord is at hand. Be careful for nothing; but in every thing by prayer and supplication* ***with thanksgiving*** *let your requests be made known unto God. And the peace of God, which passeth all understanding, shall keep your hearts and minds through Christ Jesus. Finally, brethren, whatsoever things are true, whatsoever things are honest, whatsoever things are just, whatsoever things are pure, whatsoever things are lovely, whatsoever things are of good report; if there be any virtue, and if there be any praise, think on these things. Those things, which ye have both learned, and received, and heard, and seen in me, do: and the God of peace shall be with you.*

For many years of my Christian life, I didn't understand this. My prayers were just complaints directed toward God. I didn't know prayer was supposed to be a two-way street. I told God about my problems, but I didn't acknowledge His promises or recognize His ability to perform, and so I found very little to be thankful for. As a result, my life felt out of control. I had no peace in times of trouble and experienced little joy in my salvation.

When I finally learned to pray *with* thanksgiving, my problems shrank. They didn't cease to be, but they were now in their proper perspective, and I began experiencing the peace my heart craved. I filled my mind with things that were "*true, honest, just, pure, lovely, virtuous, and of good report,*" and

suddenly, I had something to rejoice over. These are just a few of the disciplines that become rhythms of grace in your life. The simple application of them will bring great blessings into your life and all other relationships.

Chapter Sixteen

ABOUNDING WITH THANKSGIVING

You will show me the path of life; in Your presence is fullness of joy; at Your right hand are pleasures forevermore.

Psalm 16:11

A consistent diet of these spiritual disciplines helps us grow into Christlikeness and experience peace that passes understanding. They strengthen our faith and inspire endurance as we journey through life yoked together with Christ. And as we experience God's faithfulness, our hearts overflow with thanksgiving. Thanks for Him being our God. Thanks for hearing our prayers and rescuing us from trouble. Thanks for His never leaving or forsaking us despite how well we maintain these disciplines. Thanksgiving is the natural progression of faith. And while it always starts as a discipline, that rhythm of grace rewires our souls. It helps us see into the spiritual realm and uncovers all that God is doing in and through our lives.

Colossians 2:6-7 says, *"As you therefore have received Christ Jesus the Lord, so walk in Him, rooted and built up in Him and established in the faith, as you have been taught* ***abounding in it with thanksgiving.***" So few seem to get rooted and built up in Jesus or established in the faith. How do we do that? We must be taught the things regarding our faith and learn to be thankful. The things I'm sharing establish us in our faith and cause us to be rooted in Jesus so we are not shaken by the things of this world. Thanksgiving is what causes our faith to abound. Murmuring and complaining cause unbelief to abound. None of us want that!

Thanksgiving is a key element in maintaining a trouble-free heart and is God's will for us. First Thessalonians 5:17-18 says, "*Pray without ceasing. In everything give thanks; for this is the will of God in Christ Jesus concerning you.*" Notice that we are to pray without ceasing. People ask all the time, "What if nothing happens when I pray?" Keep praying. Pray until you see results. And remember to be thankful. As I said before, we don't give thanks *for* everything. That has been a misconception in the Church for years. We don't thank God *for* Satan, evil, murder, hardship, or trouble. But we do thank Him *in* it. We thank Him for His promise to perform His Word—to be with us during the trouble and to rescue us from it. We thank Him for His faithfulness.

Thanksgiving is the action of faith. James 2:17 says that faith without works is dead. Faith requires action, and one of the greatest actions of faith is an attitude of gratitude. It is thanking God for His presence and peace during our circumstances,

Murmuring and complaining cause unbelief to abound. None of us want that!

knowing that the Lord delights in showing Himself strong on our behalf.

> *For the eyes of the Lord run to and fro throughout the whole earth, to show Himself strong on behalf of those whose heart is loyal to Him.*
>
> **2 Chronicles 16:9**

God loves it when we choose to come to Him with our challenges, questions, and celebrations. He finds pleasure in "being yoked together" with us through the journey of life. But He never promised us that journey would be smooth. In John 16:33, Jesus said, *"These things I have spoken to you, that in Me you may have peace. In the world you* ***will have tribulation****; but be of good cheer, I have overcome the world."* We can count on experiencing trouble in this world, but with the right perspective, we can also be of good cheer in the middle of that trouble. Jesus also said, *"Let not your hearts be troubled; you believe in God, believe also in Me"* (John 14:1). Believing in Jesus—coming to Him and learning of Him—helps us not to let our hearts be troubled. It reminds us of all the things we can choose to be thankful for during hardship and allows us to experience God's peace that passes understanding (see Phil. 4:6). That's why fellowshipping with God in prayer and Bible study is so important. God's Word—both written and spoken—plants seeds of the Kingdom, seeds of faith, in our hearts that will bring forth a harvest of righteousness, peace, and joy in the Holy Ghost.

I don't know if you've ever realized this, but it's impossible to think on God and your problems at the same time. It's also impossible to clear your mind of all thoughts. (Though we all probably know someone who acts as if they're not thinking.) Your mind was not created for neutrality. But like the gears of a car, it also can't be in two gears at once. You can't be worried and experience peace simultaneously. Isaiah 26:3 says, *"You will keep him in perfect peace, whose mind is stayed on You, because he trusts in You."* Thinking about our problems leads to worry. Being thankful and thinking on God leads to peace (see Rom. 8:6). That's why praise and worship are so powerful, both in corporate settings and in private. It keeps our hearts and minds focused on God.

Thinking about our problems leads to worry. Being thankful and thinking on God leads to peace.

Going back to Philippians 4 (this time in the New Living Translation):

> *Don't worry about anything;*
> *instead, pray about everything. Tell God what you need, and* ***thank him*** *for all he has done. Then you will experience God's peace, which exceeds anything we can understand. His peace will guard your hearts and minds as you live in Christ Jesus. And now, dear brothers and sisters, one final thing.* ***Fix your thoughts*** *on what is true, and honorable, and right, and pure, and lovely, and admirable.*

> ***Think about*** *things that are excellent and worthy of praise.*
>
> Philippians 4:6-8

After spending time with God in prayer and thanksgiving, we are to fix our minds on things that bring peace—things that are true, honorable, right, pure, lovely, admirable, excellent, and praiseworthy. These things point to God's work in our lives. They point to His Word, both written and living; and that word is Jesus (John 1:14).

Do you feel or think you are unlovable? That's not true. You are deeply loved and of high value. Even if no one else loves you (which I don't believe is ever true), God loves you. While you were still a sinner, and an enemy of God, He loved you and sent Jesus to rescue you out of darkness (see Rom. 5:8-10; Col. 1:13). Think on that. Are you struggling with sexual sin? Fill your mind with things that are pure. Are you battling doubt? Think on God's good report. Paul had to do these things in his own life, and I've learned to do them in mine.

The ministry is full of rejection, persecution, and opposition as well as great blessings and joy. When we're overloaded or going through a problem, often the first thing we question is God's love for us. When I feel that way, I take time to get away and be with God. I meditate on how much God loves me. And that love overrides my feelings of anxiety. It casts out all worry, stress, and fear. When I'm facing a negative financial report, I remember whose report is greater. God's report says, *"But my God shall supply all your need according to his riches in glory by Christ Jesus"* (Phil. 4:19 KJV). It promises that *"God is able to make all grace abound toward you, that you, always having all sufficiency in all things, may have an abundance for every good work"* (2 Cor. 9:8). I do the same thing in a health crisis. I remind myself that healing was part of the atonement. Jesus paid for it at the same time He paid for my sins (1 Pet. 2:24). I can stand on His Word that says, *"He sent His word and healed them, and delivered them from their destructions,"* and see healing flow through my body (Ps. 107:20; Eph. 6:13).

This practice has been so beneficial to me that I no longer wait until I'm feeling worried or stressed. I take time daily to think about God's love, to fill my mind with things that are pure and honorable, and to remember God's goodness. Those thoughts guard my heart and fill it with peace. Thanksgiving for all these blessings causes our faith to abound. It fixes and sets the mind on God's goodness.

GUILT AND SHAME

As I've mentioned before, sin and guilt keep a lot of good people from experiencing peace. Whether they've found themselves stuck in a "sin cycle" or are struggling to believe that God truly forgives them when they repent; feelings of guilt, condemnation, and shame can easily overload our hearts. That's why 1 John 3:20 (KJV) says, *"For if our heart condemns us, God is greater than our heart, and knoweth all things."* Notice it's our hearts that condemn us,

It's our hearts that condemn us, not God.

not God. What part of my heart? My conscience. What does God know that many times my heart forgets? How loved and forgiven I am by God and how far God has removed my sin by the blood and sacrifice of Jesus. We have an advocate in Jesus Christ. If we confess our sins to Him, John also says, *"He is faithful and just to forgive us our sins, and to cleanse us from all unrighteousness"* (1 John 1:9). It's our conscience that needs cleansed. Dear ones, listen carefully. Those feelings of condemnation and shame are not from God. They are a scheme of Satan meant to spoil you. But we don't have to yield to his deceptions. If we mess up, we can 'fess up and receive God's forgiveness. He is faithful to forgive and cleanse our consciences (see Heb. 9:14). He is worthy of continual thanksgiving. We should abound in thanksgiving knowing the forgiveness we have in Jesus.

Don't let condemnation, guilt, embarrassment, or shame keep you from relationship with God. Don't stop going to church because you mess up or your kids go awry. Don't back away from God or stop seeking Him. Receive forgiveness and let His love and the truth of His Word deal with those feelings.

Shame has no redeemable value in our walk with God. Shame is the feeling of being unlovable or unworthy of God's love and complete forgiveness. It goes to the root of who you believe you are and is Satan's attack on your personhood. Shame convinces you to identify with sin. If you tell a lie, guilt can drive you to repent. But shame makes you a liar. Shame tells you that you are what you did—even when you *are "a new creation"* in Christ (2 Cor. 5:17). "But shouldn't I feel bad for doing wrong"? Yes. You should. That feeling of guilt has a redemptive purpose. Guilt can lead to godly sorrow which works repentance (see 2 Cor. 7:10). But we can never allow guilt, that negative feeling for behaving badly, morph into shame and negate who we are in Christ. When we sin, as believers, our conscience is defiled, but not our identity in Christ.

Your sin is not who you are, it is what you did. It's because of who you are in Christ (righteous and truly holy) that you are able now and more than willing to turn from sin. Because you are righteous in Christ, you want to act like it.

> [Jesus] *entered the Most Holy Place once for all by his own blood, thus obtaining* ***eternal redemption.*** [For if] *the blood of goats and bulls and the ashes of a heifer sprinkled on those who are ceremonially unclean* [could] *sanctify them so that they are outwardly clean. How much more, then, will the blood of Christ, who through the eternal Spirit offered himself unblemished to God,* ***cleanse our consciences*** *from acts that lead to death, so that we may serve the living God!*
>
> Hebrews 9:12-14 (NIV)

Your sin is not who you are, it is what you did.

Jesus has secured our eternal redemption. Sin cannot separate us from God's love (see Rom. 8:35-39). So, we should not allow it to overwhelm our hearts. We must learn to repent quickly and receive forgiveness before shame has a chance to take root and defile our conscience or sear it with a hot iron (see 1 Tim. 4:2). But even if our conscience be defiled, Jesus can cleanse it. He can remove the stain of shame and condemnation so we can serve (some translations say *"worship"*) the living God without tormenting fear! This is God's grace in our lives and our faith will abound in thanksgiving.

As we learn to receive God's forgiveness and understand how deeply we are loved, the joy and thanksgiving that flow from that knowledge teach us to forgive others as we have been forgiven (see Col. 3:13). All of us fail. Some in ways that are seen; some in ways that are unseen. And while the "seen" failings are more embarrassing than the unseen ones, as members of the Body of Christ, we're called to *"bear one another's burdens"* (Gal. 6:1-2). We can rest assured that if we are repentant, our sin has been dealt with through the blood of Christ. God isn't holding it over us. And neither are our brothers and sisters in Christ who have submitted themselves to God's Word. So, let's keep moving forward. Let's uproot guilt, condemnation, and shame from our hearts by meditating on God's love, mercy, and forgiveness. Let's remember His blessings; fix our minds on His promises; and abound with thanksgiving for this great salvation.

Think on and remember God's covenant promise of mercy toward us when we fail. Hebrews 8:12 reads, *"For I will be **merciful** to their unrighteousness, and their sins and lawless deeds I will remember no more."* God is not wrathful or vengeful when we sin, He is merciful. That is something to be thankful for.

We live in a dark and fallen world. And that darkness can poison our souls on a subliminal level. Coming to Jesus, staying yoked to Him, and learning of Him cleanses our souls and rights our emotions. James 4:8 says, *"Draw near to God and He will draw near to you."* This is not a legalistic promise if you do this, God will do that. God is already near you in Christ. James was talking about the free act of our will to develop rhythms of grace in our lives that help us to seek God and fix our thoughts on Him. Then, we become aware of God's presence.

> *Repent therefore and be converted, that your sins may be blotted out, so that times of refreshing may come from the presence of the Lord.*
>
> Acts 3:19

You, and only you, are responsible for developing these rhythms of grace in your life. And while the practice of each will be different from person to person, the principle remains the same. We must all find a secret place where we can be still before the Lord, where we can unload our problems and cleanse our souls by meditating on His Word. Only there, in His presence, will we experience refreshing and fullness of joy. *"Enter into his gates with thanksgiving, and into his courts with praise: be thankful unto him and bless his name. For the Lord is good; his mercy is everlasting and his truth endureth to all generations"* (Ps. 100:4-5 KJV).

Chapter Seventeen

JESUS, OUR SABBATH REST

Return to your rest, O my soul, for the
Lord has dealt bountifully with you.

Psalm 116:7

There is a rest that we, as believers, have in Christ that removes worry and fear from our hearts and fills us with peace. It is a place of safety and provision. A place of wholeness in which we commune with God as mankind once did in the Garden of Eden before sin. It is called Sabbath.

Now Sabbath, and the rest it signifies, has been limited by many just to mean a "day of worship." And while we certainly do worship God in Sabbath, the "day" on which we do so is not the focus. Sabbath is not about a day for religious observance; Sabbath is a person—Jesus Christ. Only in Him, do we find true rest, a sabbath rest.

This is not to say a day of physical rest also isn't important. It is. Jesus said, *"The Sabbath was made for man"* (Mark 2:27). God has a plan of rest that involves spirit, soul, and body. It is both spiritual and physical. Sabbath, as we have already seen, is one of the Ten Commandments, and it begins with the word "remember." Israel was to *"remember the Sabbath to keep it holy"* (Exod. 20:8). That word *remember* tells us that God instituted Sabbath before He gave the law. And while legalists of every religion demand the "keeping" of Sabbath, Scripture actually tells us we are not to just "keep it," we are to keep it *holy.* What is "holy" about the Sabbath? The Person Sabbath pointed to and testified of—Jesus, the Messiah. What is holy is God's love and provisions for us in Jesus. God's finished work in Christ to redeem us from our sins is holy. God's complete acceptance of us and forgiveness of all our sins is holy. Grace is holy.

Jesus is the substance of every shadow God revealed in the Old Testament, including the shadow of a Sabbath rest. The day the Jewish people celebrated Sabbath—Saturday—was no holier than any other day of the week. It was the rest God entered into and told His people to remember that was holy. Before the law, God revealed the concept of working six days and resting on the seventh. Genesis 2:2 says, *"And on the seventh day God ended His work which He had done, and He rested on the seventh day from all His work which He had done."* After creating the entire universe, along with the earth and all its creatures with man at the apex of it all, God rested. As I've said, that doesn't mean God was tired after all He had done. But His work was complete, it was perfect, and He was finished. So, God instituted a

Jesus is the substance of every shadow God revealed in the Old Testament, including the shadow of a Sabbath rest.

rhythm of rest to benefit the natural and spiritual life of man. In other words, God made a sustainable creation. There was an endless supply and provision for any need Adam had. Everything had seed and would reproduce after its own kind.

Under the law, God's people rested every seven days (and the land rested every seven years) as a constant reminder to "remember" the holy. And while we don't need to come under the legalism and bondage of the Sabbath as outlined in the law, we can experience its blessings of rest if we too remember to keep it holy; if we remember to come unto the person of Jesus. In 2 Peter 1:2-3 (KJV), Peter declared our provisions in Jesus: *"Grace and peace be multiplied unto you through the knowledge of God, and of Jesus our Lord, according as His divine power hath* ***given us all things*** *that pertain unto life and godliness, through the knowledge of Him that hath called us to glory."* Everything we need in our natural lives and spiritual ones is available in God's grace as we come to know His grace by revelation. It is all received by faith, faith in the finished work of Christ.

Back to the question of a day of rest. The day you choose to rest depends on the rhythm of your workweek. In the law, though the Israelites practiced Sabbath on Saturday, the priests couldn't. They were required to work in the temple and synagogues that day. So, what day did they rest? I'm not sure. But for me, Saturday is a day of prayer and preparation for Sunday's message. Sundays are a day of work as I minister the Word. So, Monday has become my day of physical rest. But Monday is not my Sabbath. My Sabbath is Jesus.

My spiritual rest is in Christ. I have ceased from my own works of self-righteousness and have entered into His work by faith (see Heb. 4:9-10). I am not laboring to earn anything from God. Neither am I laboring to save others through the preaching of the Word. My faith is in the finished work of Christ. I simply share with others the things He has shared with me. I am at peace. I have peace with God through the blood of His cross. And as far as is possible, I live at peace with all men (see Rom. 12:18). When I encounter obstacles or emotions in this life He has not called me to carry, I cast my care on the Lord. I am at rest.

I have ceased from earning or deserving anything from God. I receive by God's grace through faith. I have ceased from my own works and entered into my sabbath rest (Heb. 4:10). I have not ceased from good works. I have them but they come out of rest and faith in Jesus. I am not saved or blessed by works, but now for good works (see Eph. 2:8-10).

When Jesus secured salvation for us all, He cried, *"It is finished,"* from the cross (John 19:30). His work was done, and it was enough. We can't add to or take anything away from the cross. It was perfect. The salvation that came to the whole world through Jesus' death, burial, resurrection, and ascension were the final strokes on the Master's painting of the new creation. And just like God rested after finishing His work creating the world (first creation), Jesus sat down at the Father's right hand once His work of rescuing the world was complete (new creation) (see Heb. 1:3; 8:1; 10:12; 12:2). Now God invites us, as His children, to enter that rest

I am not saved or blessed *by* works, but now *for* good works.

by ceasing from our own works and believing in the finished work of His Son.

As Adam entered his labor in Eden from God's rest, so we now labor in God's Kingdom out of our rest in Christ. (Remember, Adam's work was to guard and garden Eden, to name the animals and care for its plants, etc. That work did not begin till the eighth day—after God rested. And yet everything he needed was available to him: an endless supply of food, water, oxygen. God had provided it all. All Adam had to do was receive.) Everything we need has been provided in Christ. We don't have to labor for salvation, healing, prosperity, favor, or blessings. We don't have to earn God's love or acceptance. It's all found in Jesus. All we have to do is come to Him, believe and receive, and enter into His rest.

There is no more fear of negative judgment. No more worry about tomorrow (see Matt. 6:34). *"Love has been perfected among us in this: that we may have boldness in the day of judgment; because as He is, so are we in this world. There is no fear in love; but perfect love casts out fear, because fear involves torment"* (1 John 4:17-18). We have no more tormenting fear of God's wrath or rejection because of Jesus and the cross. We are like Jesus. Where has this happened? Not in our bodies. Our bodies are not like Jesus'. He has an immortal body; we have mortal bodies. Our bodies are saved by hope (see Rom. 8:23-24). And while we have been promised a new body at the resurrection, our physical bodies are still subject to decay. Our carnal minds are also not as Jesus is; that's why they have to be renewed and conformed into His image. They are in the process of "being saved" (Rom. 12:2). The spirit in us is the part of us like Jesus. It is united to Christ, one spirit with the Lord (see 1 Cor. 6:17). And that is where our rest resides (see Col. 1:27).

Jesus' resurrection was the justification of all who would believe. That is why the early Church assembled on the first day of the week, Sunday. It was the day Jesus rose from the dead, and when they discovered the empty tomb. But just like Saturday, the Jewish Sabbath, was a type and shadow that pointed to the substance in Christ. It wasn't holy in and of itself; Sunday, the day most of the Church chooses to worship, isn't holy as a day either. It is simply a celebration, a reminder of what is holy—the resurrection. Colossians 2:16-17 helps us understand this. *"So let no one judge you in food or drink or regarding a festival or new moon or* ***Sabbaths****, which are a shadow of things to come, but the substance is in Christ."* The day you choose to worship isn't important to God; but remembering to keep what it testifies of is. And we are not to receive negative judgment from anyone regarding what day we worship on, or we rest.

Sunday isn't holy as a day either. It is simply a celebration, a reminder of what is holy—the resurrection.

> *Therefore, since a promise remains of* ***entering his rest****, let us fear lest any of you seem to have come short of it. For indeed the gospel was preached to us as well as to them; but the word which they heard did not profit them, not being mixed with faith in*

> *those who heard it.* ***For we who have believed do enter that rest***.
>
> Hebrews 4:1-3

Faith in God's grace is the rest we labor to enter. How do you know you've entered? Ceasing from your own works to be saved or blessed is the rest. Sabbath is not the only Old Testament shadow that Jesus fulfilled and brought substance to. The symbols were important but not above the substance. One of the simplest to understand is the sacrifice of animals. The blood sacrifices have ceased because they all pointed to the one and final sacrifice for sins—Jesus! Jesus is the lamb slain before the foundation of the world (see Rev. 13:8). He is the substance of all those pictures painted for hundreds of years. Another example, Israel's Promised Land was a land "flowing with milk and honey." It was to be their place of provision. In the New Covenant, that place is in Christ and His Kingdom. Jesus is our Promised Land; He is our provision. Jesus is also our tabernacle and temple—He is our sanctification and the place where God's glory dwells. John 2:19-21 (KJV) says, *"Jesus answered and said unto them, 'Destroy this temple, and in three days I will raise it up.' Then said the Jews, Forty and six years was this temple in building, and wilt thou rear it up in three days? But he spake of the temple of his body."* We are now God's temple as the body of Christ on the earth. Another type and shadow was the year of Jubilee. Land was returned in the year of Jubilee; debts were forgiven and slaves freed. Jesus as our Jubilee has returned us to our Father as an inheritance, our sins are forgiven, and the tyranny of sin is broken in Jesus. Jesus brings substance to all the types and shadows.

Jesus shared this sentiment many times with the Pharisees who questioned Him about healing on the Sabbath. He used both David and the priests as examples.

> *And when the Pharisees saw it, they said to him, "Look, Your disciples are doing what is not lawful to do on the Sabbath!" But He said to them, "Have you not read what David did when he was hungry, he and those who were with him: how he entered the house of God and ate the showbread which was not lawful for him to eat, nor for those who were with him, but only for the priests? Or have you not read in the law that on the Sabbath the priests in the temple profane the Sabbath, and are blameless?"*
>
> Matthew 12:2-5

When David and his men were hungry, they didn't eat the showbread out of rebellion to God's symbol. David knew that showbread was a symbol to be honored and revered. He also knew it pointed to Jesus the Bread of Life from heaven that loves us and would save us. (See John 6:32-35.) He simply knew God valued his life more than the symbol because the symbol pointed to saving his life. David knew his life was more precious than the symbol. Hosea 6:6 states, *"I desire mercy, not sacrifice."* David knew God's mercy in alleviating human suffering was more important than the letter of the law (see 1 Sam. 21:1-6). And when the priests worked in the temples on Sabbath, they did it out of obedience to God, not rebellion. They honored God with their work and were blameless. So,

Sabbath—the Jewish day pointing to the rest that was coming—was the best day on which to heal! It was a day that was holy unto the Lord. A day made for His image and to remember God's love and care for all His creation. Jesus was doing God's work (healing) on the Sabbath much like the priests in the temple were offering sacrifices that pointed to the final sacrifice of Jesus Himself.

Remember, when Jesus said, *"the Sabbath was made for man; not man for the Sabbath"* (Mark 2:27)? We weren't created for the symbols of Christ. The symbols were created for us. The Sabbath was designed to serve and benefit man, not the other way around. In the Old Testament, they pointed us toward our coming redemption. In the New Testament, they point us back to His rest (remember). Jesus continued to express God's love for us over the symbol in Matthew 12:11 (KJV), *"What man shall there be among you, that shall have one sheep, and it fall into a pit on the sabbath day, will he not lay hold on it and lift it out? Wherefore it is lawful to do well on the sabbath day."* He went on to heal a man on Saturday. God's love for us is greater than that of a sheep or the symbols pointing to substance.

Rest—both spiritual and physical—allows us to be productive. But rest takes faith. It takes faith to believe that working less can lead to prosperity and productivity. When God gave the command to rest one day out of seven, the whole world worked seven days a week, 365 days a year. And for the Israelites, Sabbath was more than just giving God every seventh day. They were also instructed to set aside the seventh and the fiftieth years, the Year of Jubilee (the 7x7th Sabbath) to allow the land to rest and to release all those who had sold their inheritance or accumulated debt. Can you imagine the amount of faith required not to work an entire year?! Yet when they chose to honor God in this way, God supernaturally prospered them and their land. Israel was blessed over every other nation on earth. Every sixth year the land produced three times the harvest of the first five years. That abundance sustained them for the sixth, seventh (while the land rested), and eighth year until what they sowed could be reaped. That's supernatural! But do you realize that promise was only a shadow of the reality that is in Christ? And just like the Israelites, we enter that promise by faith.

God's love for us is greater than that of a sheep or the symbols pointing to substance.

In Luke chapter ten, Jesus relays the struggle between works and rest while dealing with a disagreement between two sisters. Lazarus, Martha, and Mary were friends of Jesus. He often visited their home to enjoy their friendship, fellowship, and hospitality. But one time, He arrived unannounced, and Martha freaked out. She ran around the house cleaning up and preparing a seven-course meal. Her sister, Mary, on the other hand, sat at Jesus' feet and heard His Word. Mary chose to rest. Martha was *"distracted with much serving"* (Luke 10:38-39). And as she served, she became more and more stressed, until she finally exploded in frustration.

> *Lord, doesn't it seem unfair to you that my sister just sits here while I do all the work? Tell her to come and help me.*
>
> **Luke 10:40 (NLT)**

It probably wasn't wise of Martha to rebuke the Lord. Jesus responded, *"Martha, Martha."* Now, if you hear the Lord say your name twice—duck! Saul, Saul why do you persecute me? (See Acts 9:4). It's usually not very good when Jesus says your name twice.

> *You are worried and troubled about many things. But* ***one thing*** *is needed, and Mary has chosen that good part, which will not be taken away from her.*
>
> **Luke 10:41-42**

That is so powerful, and it settles the question everyone has about prioritizing work and rest because we do have to work. Work is part of the image of God in man. That's why, when we don't work, we become less than human. Work glorifies God. But, as we have seen through Adam and Christ, all our work comes out of rest.

Mary and Martha represent two different attitudes about life. Mary was Kingdom focused (she was focused on Jesus); Martha was focused on herself. Mary saw an opportunity to learn of Jesus; Martha, an opportunity to labor for Him and "prove" her love. Mary was drawn to Jesus; Martha was distracted with serving. She baked bread while Mary fed on the Bread of Life. She prepared a banquet while Mary experienced one. Mary cast her care on the Lord and experienced rest. Martha tried dumping her care on the Lord, but only grew stressed.

Work is part of the image of God in man. That's why, when we don't work, we become less than human.

Dear ones, burn out and stress do not come from *what* we do. It comes by *how* we do what we do. Mary's decision to rest, though not the only part of knowing Jesus, was the good part. And Jesus refused to take that from her. He wasn't saying it was wrong for Martha to serve or even to ask for help. He was simply bringing her service into proper focus. Serving comes out of rest.

Work, for a believer, should be a work of faith and a labor of love, not flesh or self-centeredness. Jesus was calling Martha back to the "one thing." Her company meant more to Him than her cooking. Her fellowship meant more than her floundering in the kitchen. Martha had forgotten the "one thing" that makes all other things a blessing, and she had allowed her work to become a point of pride. Mary was humble. Three times in Scripture, we find her at Jesus' feet. (Here in Luke 10:39; again when her brother died in John 11:32; and once more in John 12:3 when she worshipped by pouring perfume on Jesus.) Though Mary was known as a friend of Jesus, she remained submissive and teachable. Familiarity and friendship never clouded her love and reverence of Jesus. She kept coming to Jesus and learning of Him, and we are to follow her

We have to keep coming to Jesus. We must yoke up to Him and learn of Him to experience rest.

example. We have to keep coming to Jesus. We must yoke up to Him and learn of Him to experience rest.

The Sabbath was always meant as a day to enjoy the Lord, to let go of the six-day routine and struggles of life. It was always meant as a time to talk, fellowship, and hang out with God; to take a load off and focus on the "one thing." Sabbath is how we keep all the "other" things in their proper place. His rest is the fulfillment of and points to every rhythm of grace in our lives.

> *Come to Me, all you who labor and are heavy laden, and I will give you rest* [Sabbath]. *Take My yoke upon you and learn from Me* [sit at His feet in humility], *for I am gentle and lowly in heart* [so you can be a reflection of who He is], *and you will find rest* [Sabbath] *for your souls. For My yoke is easy and My burden is light.*
>
> Matthew 11:28-30

There is no worry or stress in God's Kingdom, no law or labor to accomplish. Grace has completed it. Now enjoy your Sabbath rest.

MORE FROM

DUANE SHERIFF

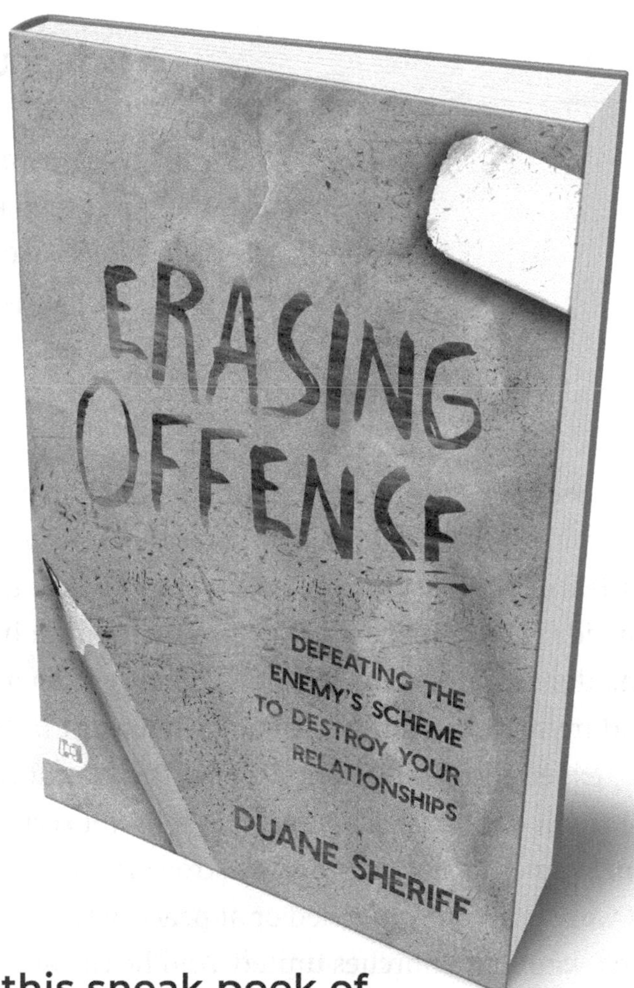

Enjoy this sneak peek of

Erasing Offense: *Defeating the Enemy's Scheme to Destroy Your Relationships*

Introduction

If you abide in my word, you are my disciples indeed. And you shall know the truth, and the truth shall make you free.

—John 8:31–32 NKJV

Learning to deal with and process offense has had a profound effect on my life, home, and ministry. Unfortunately, most people have not learned this valuable lesson. They engage in offense having no idea the damage it creates in the human heart and life. Some don't even realize they are offended! As a pastor, I often find myself explaining to people that most of the problems they experience in their marriage, in their family, or on the job are a result of offense. This shocks them, yet scripture says our enemy comes to steal, kill, and destroy (see John 10:10). He does not want us happily married or at peace with our children. He doesn't want our churches united. And he certainly doesn't want peace within our government.

Offense is one of Satan's greatest weapons. It's the root cause of marital collapse and family rifts. It's the reason politics have become so volatile. It's also why many believers remain immature and churches spiral into dysfunction.

Satan thrives on division, strife, contention, and offense. He uses offense to steal the Word of God from our hearts and create chaos in our lives. Even ministers fall into his trap. Offense amongst church leaders and staff creates a "staff infection" that hinders the move and power of God by opening the door to envy, strife, and *"every evil work"* (James 3:16).

The dangers of offense are far-reaching—offense steals our peace, destroys relationships, and can ultimately warp our personalities—yet most people have not been taught how to process it. Thankfully, the Word of God gives us the tools we need to recognize, process, and avoid offense. Psalm 119:165 says, *"Great peace have they which love thy law: and nothing shall offend them."*

You'd probably be hard-pressed to find someone in your circle of influence who does not get offended. But the Bible says, if we truly love God's Word and embrace its teaching, we'll have great peace. Not just peace, but great peace. Nothing will be able to offend us. Imagine that. Imagine living at peace with your spouse. At peace with your children. Imagine having peace in your workplace. Peace in your school and with other believers. Dear ones, it is possible.

I have lived at peace with those in my circle of relationships for decades. Since God has made peace with me through the blood of His cross, I can live at peace, not only with God, but with my fellow man. I can live in peace with my wife and children. I can have peace in my church, peace with my staff. I don't have to live in strife. I don't have to be jealous of other ministry gifts. I don't have to feel uncomfortable around those who've wronged me. How? It starts by loving God's Word (see Psalm 119:165).

None of us—from the least to the greatest—is immune to the temptation of offense. You'll probably have opportunity to get offended just reading this book! But we don't have to live in offense. If we understand the deadliness of offense and learn to recognize how Satan uses it to steal the fruit of our righteousness, we will find it easier to deal with and overcome offense in our lives.

In this book, I'll show you how. I'll define offense and reveal its long-term effects using both biblical and personal examples. I'll teach you how to discern offense in general and identify the offenses in your own life. I'll show you how to process offense and take the necessary steps to overcome it so you can reverse its effects in your life and family. With time, as you abide in and love God's Word, these truths will set you free.

CHAPTER ONE

The Danger of Offense

An offended friend is harder to win back than a fortified city. Arguments separate friends like a gate locked with bars.
—Proverbs 18:19 NLT

Offense is one of the most dangerous heart conditions in our society, affecting believers and nonbelievers alike. But offense may not be what you think.

All of us face opportunities to become offended. Understanding the dangers associated with offense helps us resist this temptation. But most people have not been taught the deadliness of offense, so they suffer its affects unwittingly. In order to live the blessed and fruitful life Jesus called us to, we have to remain void of offense—whether that means resisting the temptation of offense or repenting of an offense we've taken.

Years ago, when my wife, Sue, and I were still young in ministry, some friends asked us to dinner to give us a "word from the Lord." At this point in our ministry, we were traveling and had begun distributing free messages, but offerings were not yet covering our expenses—let alone a salary. And quite honestly, we were just as excited about the free meal as we were the word from the Lord.

Dinner went well, and we were enjoying fellowship when this couple finally got around to giving us the "word from the Lord." It went something like this: "The Lord has shown us that three wolves are coming into your ministry who are endeavoring to devour you." Talk about unsettling! Suddenly, the free meal began turning in my stomach.

I had lots of questions about the word. I wanted details like who, when, how, and where. But the couple had no idea. They just gave us the word the Lord had given them and told us to be prepared. Perhaps even more puzzling to me—Sue didn't seem to be concerned. As soon as we got in the car, I asked her what she thought of the word. "Who could possibly want to hurt our ministry?"

My sweet, loving wife looked at me as serious as can be and responded, "I don't know who the third wolf is, but two of them were sitting at the table with us."

I couldn't believe my ears! After recovering our car from the bar ditch, I said, "Honey! How could you say such a thing? They're our friends!" I wasn't trying to condemn Sue, but I could not fathom this couple doing such a thing. After all, they were the ones who had given us the word. Could they really be party to the destruction of our ministry? Sue was unmoved by my outburst. She was actually operating in the discerning of spirits and discerned that the word was coming out of their own hearts.

Two weeks later, that couple and a local pastor in our prayer circle called me a false prophet from the pulpit. They instructed everyone in their congregation to burn my cassette tapes (yes, it was a long time ago!) and never listen to me again. In that moment, I had opportunity to take offense. But had I done so, that offense could have ruined our lives and destroyed the fruitfulness of our ministry.

Sue, too, could have taken offense—at me—for not trusting her discernment in the matter. And that offense would have brought turmoil to our marriage. Instead, we prayed together over it. We judged our own hearts, reminded ourselves of what God had called us to do, and forgave them. We continued to teach the Word as God instructed us and distributed our messages free of charge. As a result, our ministry became more and more fruitful, but over the years, theirs became fruitless.

Dear ones, no person can cause you or your ministry to fail. No one can cause you to become fruitless. Only you can do that by harboring offense. And while this experience was painful, I learned something important—always listen to Sue!

You may have never thought about this, but Christians don't really produce fruit. Christians are the bride of Christ. We are in a husband-wife type of relationship with Jesus, and just like a wife bears children, we—as Christ's bride—bear fruit. Jesus is the one who produces it. Fruit is the by-product of a heart in right relationship with Jesus. It is the proof of our faith working together with His grace.

In Mark 4, Jesus used the Parable of the Sower to teach us how God's Word produces fruit in our hearts and lives. In it, Jesus describes a man who went out to sow seed. As he was sowing, the man's seed fell on different types of ground and produced different results. When Jesus' disciples approached Him about the meaning of this parable, He said that God's Word is like seed and our hearts are like the ground. As God's Word abides in the ground of our hearts, we bear fruit.

So why don't all Christians bear the same amount of fruit in their lives? According to Jesus' parable, the problem lies with the ground. God's Word, the seed, is constant. But of the four types of ground Jesus listed in His parable, only one brought forth fruit *"some thirtyfold, some sixty, and some a hundred"* times what was sown (Mark 4:8, 20 NKJV). Any lack of fruit was not due to the seed, but rather to the condition of the ground. Today, when you see Christians displaying different kinds and amounts of fruit, the variable is always the ground of their hearts.

FOUR TYPES OF GROUND

The first type of ground mentioned in Mark lay "by the wayside." This ground was literally on the side of the farmer's field. It was the path people walked to avoid compacting the farmer's prepared soil and tender, growing plants. Jesus likened this ground to His hearers with hard hearts. *"And these are they by the wayside, where the word is sown; but when they have heard, Satan cometh immediately, and taketh away the word that was sown in their hearts"* (Mark 4:15).

In Matthew's account of this same parable, Jesus said, *"When any one heareth the word of the kingdom, and* ***understandeth it not,*** *then cometh the wicked one, and catcheth away that which was sown in his heart..."* (Matthew 13:19). When we hear but do not understand God's Word, Satan steals the seed from our hearts. As a result, we bear no fruit.

ABOUT DUANE SHERIFF

Duane Sheriff is the founding pastor and senior elder of Victory Life Church, a growing multi-campus church where he served as the senior pastor for over 35 years. His passion is to see people discover their true identity and help them grow in Christ. From the inception of his teaching ministry, this passion has compelled him to make his teachings available free. He enjoys hunting and spending time with his family, especially the grandchildren.

For additional information and resources
by Duane Sheriff, visit
www.pastorduane.com

In the Right Hands, This Book Will Change Lives!

Most of the people who need this message will not be looking for this book. To change their lives, you need to **put a copy of this book in their hands.**

Our ministry is constantly seeking methods to find the people who need this anointed message to change their lives. **Will you help us reach these people?**

Extend this ministry by sowing 3 books, 5 books, 10 books, or more today, and become a life changer! Your generosity will be part of catalyzing the Great Awakening that many have been prophesying and praying for.